The SEVEN CHURCHES of ASIA

Bill Humble
Ian Fair

Gospel Advocate Company
P. O. Box 150
Nashville, Tennessee 37202

Design by Brad Roberts and Susan Barnes.

All photos courtesy of Bill Humble.

Unless otherwise indicated, Scripture quotations are from the Revised Standard Version, copyright 1971, by Division of Christian Education of the National Council of the Churches of Christ of the United States of America.

Published by Gospel Advocate Company
PO Box 150, Nashville, TN 37202.

ISBN 0-89225-457-2

Table of Contents

# Foreword

It's the next best thing to being there! As I viewed the video series by Dr. Bill Humble and Dr. Ian Fair on the Seven Churches of Asia, that was my sentiment over and over. As these men and their Turkish guide, Husnu Ovacik, walked among the ruins of civilizations long past, I marveled at how they wove together the ancient and the contemporary. My eyes were opened to biblical truths that I had never seen before about the mysterious and haunting Seven Churches of Asia mentioned in Revelation 2 and 3.

Bill and Ian are the perfect pair to make biblical history come alive. Bill is a superb archaeologist and biblical historian. Ian is a specialist in the book of Revelation. Both have spent most of their lives at Abilene Christian University, teaching students about God's Word and its relevance for all times and all cultures. The visual artistry of the camera is enhanced to its fullest through the talents of Dr. Dutch Hoggatt, also on the ACU faculty.

It is important for us and for our children to know the Christian legacy that has been left to us by believers of the past. The ancient ruins of these cities remind us about a time nearly 2,000 years ago. Their circumstances and their problems, however, are as contemporary as today's newspaper headlines.

For years to come, these videos will be useful and instructive for people in church settings, in academic classrooms and in homes. I am thankful that we now have this excellent teaching tool that combines so well the visual, oral and written story of God's message to churches, both ancient and modern.

Royce Money, Ph.D.
President
Abilene Christian University

Revelation 1-3

1 The revelation of Jesus Christ, which God gave him to show to his servants what must soon take place; and he made it known by sending his angel to his servant John, {2} who bore witness to the word of God and to the testimony of Jesus Christ, even to all that he saw. {3} Blessed is he who reads aloud the words of the prophecy, and blessed are those who hear, and who keep what is written therein; for the time is near.

{4} John to the seven churches that are in Asia:

Grace to you and peace from him who is and who was and who is to come, and from the seven spirits who are before his throne, {5} and from Jesus Christ the faithful witness, the first-born of the dead, and the ruler of kings on earth.

To him who loves us and has freed us from our sins by his blood {6} and made us a kingdom, priests to his God and Father, to him be glory and dominion for ever and ever. Amen. {7} Behold, he is coming with the clouds, and every eye will see him, every one who pierced him; and all tribes of the earth will wail on account of him. Even so. Amen.

{8} "I am the Alpha and the Omega," says the Lord God, who is and who was and who is to come, the Almighty.

{9} I John, your brother, who share with you in Jesus the tribulation and the kingdom and the patient endurance, was on the island called Patmos on account of the word of God and the testimony of Jesus. {10} I was in the Spirit on the Lord's day, and I heard behind me a loud voice like a trumpet {11} saying, "Write what you see in a book and send it to the seven churches, to Ephesus and to Smyrna and to Pergamum and to Thyatira and to Sardis and to Philadelphia and to Laodicea."

{12} Then I turned to see the voice that was speaking to me, and on turning I saw seven golden lampstands, {13} and in the midst of the lampstands one like a son of man, clothed with a long robe and with a golden girdle round his breast; {14} his head and his hair were white as white wool, white as snow; his eyes were like a flame of fire, {15} his feet were like burnished bronze, refined as in a furnace, and his voice was like the sound of many waters; {16} in his right hand he held seven stars, and from his mouth issued a sharp two-edged sword, and his face was like the sun shining in full strength.

{17} When I saw him, I fell at his feet as though dead. But he laid his right hand upon me, saying, "Fear not, I am the first and last, {18} and the living one; I died, and behold I am alive for evermore, and I have the keys of Death and Hades. {19} Now write what you see, what is and what is to take place hereafter. {20} As for the mystery of the seven stars which you saw in my right hand, and the seven golden lampstands, the seven stars are the angels of the seven churches and the seven lampstands are the seven churches.

THE LETTER TO EPHESUS

2 "To the angel of the church in Ephesus write: 'The words of him who holds the seven stars in his right hand, who walks among the seven golden lampstands.

{2} " 'I know your works, your toil and your patient endurance, and now you cannot bear evil men but have tested those who call themselves apostles but are not, and found them to be false; {3} I know you are enduring patiently and bearing up my name's sake, and you have not grown weary. {4} But I have this against you, that you have abandoned the love you had at first. {5} Remember then from what you have fallen, repent and do the works you did at first. If not, I will come to you and remove your lampstand from its place, unless you repent. {6} Yet this you have, you hate the works of the Nicolaitans, which I also hate. {7} He who has an ear, let him hear what the Spirit says to the churches. To him who conquers I will grant to eat of the tree of life, which is in the paradise of God.'

THE LETTER TO SYMRNA

{8} "And to the angel of the church in Smyrna write: 'The words of the first and the last, who died and came to life.

{9} " 'I know your tribulation and your poverty (but you are rich) and the slander those who say that they are Jews and are not, but are a synagogue of Satan. {10} Do not fear what you are about to suffer. Behold, the devil is about to throw some of you into prison, that you may be tested, and for ten days you will have tribulation. Be faithful unto death, and I will give you the crown of life. {11} He who has an ear, let him hear what the Spirit says to the churches. He who conquers shall not be hurt by the second death.'

THE LETTER TO PERGAMUM

{12} "And to the angel of the church in Pergamum write: 'The words of him who has the sharp two-edged sword.

{13} " 'I know where you dwell, where Satan's throne is; you hold fast my name and you did not deny my faith even in the days of Antipas my witness, my faithful one, who was killed among you, where Satan dwells. {14} But I have a few things against you: you have some there who hold the teaching of Balaam, who taught Balak to put a stumbling block before the sons of Israel, that they might eat food sacrificed to idols and practice immorality. {15} So you also have some who hold the teaching of the Nicolaitans. {16} Repent then. If not, I will come to you soon and war against them with the sword of my mouth. {17} He who has an ear, let him hear what the Spirit says to the churches. To him who conquers I will give some of the hidden manna, and I will give him a white stone, with a new name written on the stone which no one knows except him who receives it.'

THE LETTER TO THYATIRA
{18} "And to the angel of the church in Thyatira write: 'The words of the Son of God, who has eyes like a flame of fire, and whose feet are like burnished bronze.

{19} " 'I know your works, your love and faith and service and patient endurance, and that your latter works exceed the first. {20} But I have this against you, that you tolerate the woman Jezebel, who calls herself a prophetess and is teaching and beguiling my servants to practice immorality and to eat food sacrificed to idols. {21} I gave her time to repent, but she refuses to repent of her immorality. {22} Behold, I will throw her on a sickbed, and those who commit adultery with her I will throw into great tribulation, unless they repent of her doings; {23} and I will strike her children dead. And all the churches shall know that I am he who searches mind and heart, and I will give to each of you as your works deserve. {24} But to the rest of you in Thyatira, who do not hold this teaching, who have not learned what some call the deep things of Satan, to you I say, I do not lay upon you any other burden; {25} only hold fast what you have until I come. {26} Hw who conquers and who keeps my works untill the end, I will give him power over the nations, {27} and he shall rule them with a rod of iron, as when earthen pots are broken in pieces, even as I myself have received power from my Father; {28} and I will give him the morning star. {29} He who has an ear, let him hear what the Spirit says to the churches.'

THE LETTER TO SARDIS

3 "And to the angel of the church in Sardis write: 'The words of him who has the seven spirits of God and the seven stars.

" 'I know your works; you have the name of being alive, and you are dead. {2} Awake, and strengthen what remains and is on the point of death, for I have not found your works perfect in the sight of my God. {3} Remember then what you received and heard; keep that, and repent. If you will not awake, I will come like a thief, and you will not know at what hour I will come upon you. {4} Yet you have still a few names in Sardis, people who have not soiled their garments; and they shall walk with me in white, for they are worthy. {5} He who conquers shall be clad thus in white garments, and I will not blot his name out of the book of life; I will confess his name before my Father and before his angels. {6} He who has an ear, let him hear what the Spirit says to the churches.'

THE LETTER TO PHILADELPHIA

{7} "And to the angel of the church in Philadelphia write: 'The words of the holy one, the true one, who has the key of David, who opens and no one shall shut, who shuts and no one opens.

{8} " 'I know your works. Behold, I have set before you an open door, which no one is able to shut; I know that you have but little power, and yet you have kept my word and have not denied my name. {9} Behold, I will make those of the synagogue of Satan who say that they are Jews and are not, but lie — behold, I will make them come and bow down before your feet, and learn that I have loved you. {10} Because you have kept my word of patient endurance, I will keep you from the hour of trial which is coming on the whole world, to try those who dwell upon the earth. {11} I am coming soon; hold fast what you have, so that no one may seize your crown. {12} He who conquers, I will make him a pillar in the temple of my God; never shall he go out of it, and I will write on him the name of my God, and the name of the city of my God, the new Jerusalem which comes down from my God out of heaven, and my own new name. {13} He who has an ear, let him hear what the Spirit says to the churches.'

THE LETTER TO LAODICEA

{14} "And to the angel of the church in Laodicea write: 'The words of the Amen, the faithful and true witness, the beginning of God's creation.

{15} " 'I know your works: you are neither cold nor hot. Would that you were cold or hot! {16} So, because you are lukewarm, and neither cold nor hot, I will spew you out of my mouth. {17} For you say, I am rich, I have prospered, and I need nothing; not knowing that you are wretched, pitiable, poor, blind, and naked. {18} Therefore I counsel you to buy from me gold refined by fire, that you may be rich, and white garments to clothe you and to keep the shame of your nakedness from being seen, and salve to anoint your eyes, so that you may see. {19} Those whom I love, I reprove and chasten; so be zealous and repent. {20} Behold, I stand at the door and knock; if any one hears my voice and opens the door, I will come in to him and eat with him, and he with me. {21} He who conquers, I will grant him to sit with me on my throne, as I myself conquered and sat down with my Father on his throne. {22} He who has an ear, let him hear what the Spirit says to the churches.' "

1

Asia:
The Roman Province

The letters of Paul have many references to "the province of Asia," and the "seven churches of Asia" are well-known to students of the New Testament. But the word "Asia" is confusing. We think of Asia as the vast continent stretching from Turkey and the Aegean Sea eastward to China and Japan. Ancient writers, including Josephus and the Greek historians, often used Asia in this sense. However, in the New Testament Asia nearly always refers to the Roman province located in the western part of what is now Turkey, earlier called Asia Minor or Anatolia. The seven churches were all located in this Roman province of Asia. We will return to Roman Asia later in this chapter, but first we need a brief overview of the earlier history of western Asia Minor and the beginnings of the cities where the seven churches would later be located.

The two chief powers in Asia Minor during the second millennium B.C. were the city of Troy and the Hittite Empire. Ancient Troy was situated on the Aegean Sea in northwest Asia Minor, about 50-100 miles north of the area where the seven churches would later be located. Homer's epic poems, *The Iliad* and *The Odyssey*, tell about Helen of Troy, the war between Troy and the Greeks, and Achilles and the Trojan horse. Many 19th-century scholars regarded Homer's poems as mythical and doubted whether a real Troy ever existed. But a German business-man-turned-archaeologist, Heinrich Schliemann, was convinced that Homer's accounts were historical. Using them as a starting point, he found Troy. Heinrich excavated the site from 1870-1890, and discovered priceless gold artifacts. Later excavations have shown that Troy was an important city for many centuries before its destruction by the Greeks about 1250 B.C.

The Hittite Empire dominated the heartland of Asia Minor from 1750 B.C. until about 1200 B.C. The Hittite capital was Hattusas (modern Bogazkoy), located about 500 miles east of Troy and the Aegean Sea. The Old Testament has about 40 references to the Hittites. When Sarah died, Abraham purchased the Cave of Machpaleh from the Hittites as a burial place (Genesis 23). Esau married Hittite wives (Genesis 36:1-3), as did Solomon (1 Kings 11:1). And David ordered the death of Uriah the Hittite, Bathsheba's husband (2 Samuel 11:1-25).

Like Troy, the very existence of the Hittites was once questioned, since no historical references to them could be found outside the Old Testament. This skepticism ended early in the 20th century when Hugo Winkler discovered walled city of Hattusas. Thanks to the recovery of 10,000 clay tablets in a royal archive at Hattusas, we know a great deal about the Hittites. We know, for example, that in 1286 B.C. Pharaoh Ramses II and the Hittites fought a great battle on the Orontes River in Syria. Neither side won a clear victory, so 15 years later a peace treaty was negotiated between the Egyptians and the Hittites. The clay tablet on which this treaty is written is the oldest non-aggression pact between two nations that has been discovered. That tablet is now on display at the Istanbul museum.

Sometime after 1200 B.C. nomadic tribes from inner Asia swept into Asia Minor, the Hittite Empire collapsed, and a dark age followed. Little is known about what happened in Asia Minor for the next two or three centuries. However, it was sometime during this dark age, probably around 1000 B.C., that the first Greek settlements were planted on the western coast of Asia Minor. The Ionian colonists from Greece sailed across the 200-mile-wide Aegean Sea and settled at Ephesus, Miletus, Smyrna and Magnesias. They also occupied many of the islands lying off the coast including Mitylene, Rhodes and perhaps Patmos. Thus, the Greek language and culture were planted in western Asia Minor a thousand years before the seven churches came into existence.

The kingdom of Lydia emerged as the dominant power in western Asia Minor during the seventh century B.C. Sardis, located on the Pactolus River, was the Lydian capital. When gold was discovered in the Pactolus, Sardis became the wealthiest city in the world. The first coins were minted there. Croesus (560-546 B.C.) was the most famous king of Lydia and is still remembered for his legendary wealth in gold.

King Croesus wanted to attack Persia, but he was not sure he could defeat such a powerful enemy. According to Herodatus, Croesus sought counsel from the oracle of Apollo at Delphi in Greece. The oracle told him, "If you cross the River Halys, you will destroy a great empire." The unfortunate Croesus misinterpreted this enigmatic advice. When he attacked Persia, Croesus destroyed his own kingdom — not Persia. King Cyrus of Persia defeated the Lydians and laid siege to the Sardis acropolis. The acropolis was so lofty — 1,500 feet above the city — and so strongly fortified that everyone assumed that it was impregnable to attack, but it fell to the Persians. This ended the kingdom of Lydia, but Sardis survived and continued to be an important city into the New Testament period.

The Greek cities of western Asia Minor soon found that the Persians were harsher taskmasters than the Lydians had been, and their resentment sparked revolt. The uprising began at Miletus in 499 B.C. and included all the Greek cities along the coast, aided and abetted by Athens. The Persians decided to punish Athens. Their armies crossed the Hellespont and invaded Greece but were defeated at the historic battle of Marathon. Ten years later a new Persian king, Xerxes, tried again. Using Sardis as his headquarters, he assembled a huge army and navy, attacked Greece again, and burned and looted Athens. But the Greeks turned Xerxes back at the naval battle of Salamis, and the Persians had to retreat to Asia Minor.

Alexander the Great came to the throne of Macedon 150 years later and united Greece against the Persians. He crossed the Hellespont in 334 B.C. with an army of 34,000 and defeated the Persians at the Granicus River north of Pergamum. Alexander next turned his armies southward. He captured the Persian headquarters at Sardis, and then Ephesus. Soon all of Asia Minor was under Alexander's control. The Persian empire crumbled, and a new Hellenistic world order with Greek language and culture replaced it throughout the East. After Alexander's death at Babylon in 323 B.C. a line of Greek kings, the Seleucids, ruled Asia Minor for more than a century. The Seleucids, in turn, were defeated by the Romans and western Asia Minor fell under Roman control.

Pergamum was the leading city in western Asia Minor around 200 B.C. Its kings, the Attalid dynasty, had allied themselves with Rome against the Seleucids. After defeating the Seleucids, the Romans treated Pergamum as a faithful ally and allowed its kings to rule western Asia Minor. However, the Pergamum king, Attalus III, realized that his kingdom could not maintain its independence against the growing power of Rome, so he voluntarily bequeathed his kingdom to the Romans in 133 B.C.

The Roman Province of Asia

The Romans called their new province "Asia" since they had known the Attalids as the "kings of Asia." Initially, Asia included all the lands along the Aegean coast of Asia Minor and many of the Aegean islands including Rhodes and Patmos. In 116 B.C., parts of Phrygia to the east were incorporated into Asia. Thus, by New Testament times the Roman province of Asia included all the lands from the Aegean eastward to Galatia (250 miles) and from Bithynia in the north to Lycia in the south (225 miles) — an area of about 56,000 square miles or slightly larger than Arkansas. The western part of Roman Asia had many important cities: Hierapolis, Colossae, Miletus, Aphrodisias, Priene, and others along with the seven cities of Revelation.

Sir William Ramsey, the 19th-century British archaeologist who did early excavating in Asia Minor, was the first to note that the letters to the seven churches in Revelation 2-3 are arranged in the order that a messenger would have visited the seven cities. Had a young disciple of John been entrusted with delivering the letters, he would have sailed from Patmos to Ephesus, the largest and most important of the cities in New Testament times. From Ephesus he would have journeyed 100 miles north to Smyrna and Pergamum. He would have left Pergamum traveling southeast to Thyatira and Sardis, then on to Philadelphia and Laodicea, a distance of 150 miles. It was 100 miles west from Laodicea back to Ephesus, and the messenger's 350-mile triangle would have been complete.[1]

---

1. The chapters in this book and the accompanying video do not follow the same order as the letters are presented in Revelation 2-3. The amount of archaeological and background information about each city and church varies widely. The order followed in this study is an attempt to present the information in segments that are relatively uniform in size.

The Romans showed Pergamum many favors out of gratitude for King Attalus bequeathing his kingdom to Rome. They made Pergamum the capital of Asia, until supplanted by Ephesus a century later. Pergamum also became the center of emperor worship in Asia. It was the first city granted permission to worship the living emperor as god, and a temple dedicated to Rome and the Emperor Augustus was built in 29 B.C. Archaeologists have not found this temple, but they have found coins with pictures of the temple. Emperor worship spread from Pergamum to the other cities of Asia. By the end of the first century, when Revelation was written, emperor worship was a life-and-death challenge to Christians and provided the historical context for Revelation.

The language and culture of Roman Asia were predominately Greek. Some of the Greek cities along the Aegean coast had been there for 1,000 years. After Alexander the Great's conquests, all of Asia Minor became an integral part of the Greek world and the rulers made deliberate efforts to Hellenize their territories. Philadelphia, for example, was the newest of the seven cities of Asia. It was founded by King Attalus II of Pergamum about 150 B.C. for the purpose of spreading Greek culture into the heartland of Asia Minor.

Roman Asia was also home to many non-Greeks. The descendants of many earlier races in the region — Lydians, Carians, Armenians, Hittites, and others — had more or less absorbed the Hellenistic culture around them. A significant Jewish population was also found in Asia. Asian Jews were in Jerusalem for Pentecost (Acts 2:9), and it was Jews from Asia who disputed with Stephen (Acts 6:9). Two of the seven letters, those to Smyrna and Philadelphia, reflect bitter hostility between the Jews and Christians in those cities. In Sardis, archaeologists have discovered and restored the largest, ancient Jewish synagogue ever found.

It has been estimated that the total population of Asia may have been reached 4.6 million by the second century A.D. Asia may have been the wealthiest province in the Roman Empire in New Testament times. The valleys along the rivers were fertile, and Asia produced cereal grains, grapes, fruit and nuts. The area was rich in building materials including good timber, fine marble and building stone. Although the gold and silver of earlier centuries had been depleted, lead and other minerals were still being mined. The area around Laodicea was noted for its fine black sheep and luxurious wool clothing.

Asia was the natural land bridge between the Aegean world and the Mesopotamian world to the east. The Asian cities that stood astride those trade routes — Ephesus, Smyrna and Laodicea — grew rich from the trade.

Less than a century after Rome gained control of Asia, the statesman Cicero wrote of Asia's wealth: "In the richness of its soil, in the variety of its products, in the extent of its pastures, and in the number of its exports, it surpasses all other lands."

The religions in Asia were almost as varied as the people and products. The Jews were firm in their faith in the one God of Abraham, Isaac and Jacob, even though they had become Hellenized in their language and culture. The other people of Asia worshiped the whole pantheon of Greco-Roman gods and goddesses. An Asian fertility goddess, often represented as a many-breasted image, had been worshiped in the Ephesus region from ancient times. When the Greeks came, this ancient faith was assimilated into the worship of Artemis (also known as the Roman goddess Diana). The temples to Artemis at Ephesus and Sardis were two of the largest buildings in the Hellenistic world. The Temple of Apollo at Didyma, where the oracle spoke, rivaled the one at Delphi in Greece. The temple-hospital to Asclepias at Pergamum was second in magnitude only to the great sanctuary at Epidarus, Greece. Zeus and Athena also had their temples at Pergamum.

Roman Asia was also a center for emperor worship. It began at Pergamum when Rome granted permission to build a temple to the emperor in 29 B.C. Pergamum remained the center for emperor worship through New Testament times. Emperor worship spread rapidly as other cities vied for the honor of building temples to the emperors. The people who already worshiped Zeus and the other Greek gods and goddesses found it easy to add an emperor or two to their list of deities. But for the

Christians, emperor worship sometimes brought them face-to-face with cruel choices and even death. The seven letters in Revelation, even the whole book, cannot be understood apart from this context of emperor worship.

The Seven Churches

The gospel of Jesus Christ began to be proclaimed in Asia sometime around the middle of the first century A.D. Jews from Asia were in Peter's audience on Pentecost (Acts 2:9). If some of these Asian Jews were among the 3,000 baptized on that day, they probably returned home to Asia as witnesses for Jesus. On Paul's second missionary journey, he was forbidden by the Spirit to preach in Asia (Acts 16:6). Yet Paul and his traveling companions, Silas and Timothy, had to cross Asia to reach Troas from whence the Spirit directed them to Macedonia. Later, on the second journey, Paul stopped briefly at Ephesus and left Priscilla and Aquila there, intending to return later if it was the Lord's will (Acts 18:18-21).

Paul did return to Ephesus on the third journey and lived there for three years (Acts 20:31). He taught "in public and from house to house testifying both to Jews and to Greeks of repentance to God and of faith in our Lord Jesus Christ (Acts 20:20-21). The New Testament does not say that Paul preached in other cities of Asia. The churches in the other cities of Asia were probably planted during this time. We will never know whether Paul himself visited such cities as Pergamum and Laodicea or whether the church-planting was the work of fellow Christians.

Near the end of Paul's three-year ministry at Ephesus, he wrote that "a wide door for effective work has opened to me" but added that "there are many adversaries" (1 Corinthians 16:9). He said he had "fought with beasts at Ephesus" (1 Corinthians 15:32). This is probably a figurative description of his opposers, but it may be possible that he had actually faced wild animals in the gladiatorial arena. After leaving Ephesus, Paul recalled his struggles there: "For we were so utterly, unbearably crushed that we despaired of life itself. Why, we felt that we had received the sentence of death" (2 Corinthians 1:8-9).

Just a few years later while imprisoned in Rome, Paul wrote the New Testament epistle of Ephesians. Many scholars believe that it was not intended exclusively for the Ephesian church but was a general letter for all the Asian churches. The letter begins with a greeting to the saints in Ephesus, but the words "in Ephesus" are missing in the oldest Greek manuscripts. The letter also lacks the personal messages one would expect if it were written to brethren Paul knew intimately. So if Ephesians was a circular letter, it might have been carried — like Revelation was later — first to Ephesus, then to Smyrna and Pergamum and the other churches of Asia.

Toward the end of the first century, emperor worship was confronting the Christians in Asia with a life-and-death choice: confess that Caesar was Lord or be charged with treason. The Emperor Domitian (A.D. 81-96), who was worshiped as a god at a great temple in Ephesus, exiled the elderly John to Patmos. John was in the Spirit on the Lord's Day and heard a voice like a trumpet, which said, "Write what you see in a book and send it to the seven churches" (Revelation 1:11). The seven short but important letters follow in Revelation 2-3.

As we examine each of these letters, remember that they were written to real people in real places. Consider whether the problems they faced are similar to the problems we face. Remember that the Lord's admonitions and promises are true for all Christians, including the church today.   **BH**

2

Ephesus

Bill Humble:

The seven churches of Asia! When we read those words, we think of Revelation chapters one through three: The triumphant Lord walking in the midst of His church and addressing letters through John to the seven churches of Asia. Ian Fair and I are going to take you to visit those seven churches. The reason is simple. Now, Ephesus and Smyrna and Laodicea are names in your Bible, just names. But we believe that if they become real cities with real people who were New Testament Christians in the long ago, the Bible will spring to life and become a living book.

The Lord's first letter was to the church in Ephesus, and that's where we are — at the great theater in Ephesus. We will come back to this theater later.

Ephesus was a walled city in New Testament times, and the Curetes Street ran from the main gate, on the east, to the heart of the city. Some sections of the ancient walls can still be seen on the crest of the hills surrounding the city.

Today, as we walk down the Curetes Street, we see evidence everywhere of the greatness of this ancient city. The street was lined with marble columns, sidewalks and shops, fountains, and temples to the emperors. Ephesus was the fourth largest city in the Roman world with a population of 250,000.

Ephesus is important in the New Testament because two of the apostles, Paul and John, lived here and wrote letters to their fellow Christians here. Paul lived here for three years on his third missionary journey and later wrote the book of Ephesians from Rome. Forty years later, after John's exile on Patmos ended, he came to Ephesus and died here. So as we follow these ancient streets, we are walking in the footsteps of both Paul and John.

When visitors like Paul came into Ephesus on the Curetes Street, the first public buildings they came to were in the state agora, which was the civic center of the city. The town hall was here. The agora also had a small theater called the Odeion. It was used for musical programs and for meetings of the city council. The Odeion has been excavated and restored by archaeologists from Austria.

Ephesus boasted many public baths for its citizens, and one of these was located on the Curetes Street. It was a large building with several rooms and massive walls. It was a typical Roman bath with hot and cold rooms. The small columns that supported the floor in the hot room, or caldarium, can still be seen. And the clay water mains are still in place. These baths were in use in the first century, but they were enlarged later.

Husnu Ovacik:

The Scholastica baths were reconstructed in the fourth century, but the Roman baths existed from the beginning of the first century. What Scholastica did, being a very wealthy lady, was reconstruct and enlarge the whole complex. This was in the fourth century.

Bill Humble:

Scholastica, who gave the money to enlarge the baths, was a Christian. The grateful city put a statue of her in the baths.

There was a row of shops on the opposite side of the Curetes Street. These were separated from the street by a row of columns and a sidewalk. The sidewalk was made of mosaics, and many of them are still in place. These mosaics, along with many fragments of marble carvings from the temples and other buildings, show that Ephesus was a city of remarkable beauty in New Testament times.

Temple of Hadrian in Ephesus, built about A.D. 138.

This temple, dedicated to the emperor Hadrian, was next to the baths on the Curetes Street. Ephesus was Hadrian's favorite city, and he made it the Roman capital of Asia. The front arch of this temple has his name and Tyche, the goddess of good fortune. The second arch has Medusa with her hair turned into snakes. The temple is small, but architects have called it the most beautiful edifice in the city.

Even though this temple was built a few years after Revelation was written, it shows why the book was written — to warn Christians of the trials ahead. In apocalyptic language, Revelation pictures Rome as the enemy — a beast, a harlot — demanding that the emperor be worshiped as god.

Ian, I know that emperor worship was a big problem to the Christians who lived in Asia. Can you tell me why?

Ian Fair:

Yes, it's not that emperor worship was peculiar to this particular period. It had been taking place for centuries. But for the first time, toward the close of the first century, believers — both Jews and Christians — were being persecuted when they refused to worship the emperor.

Bill Humble:

Are there temples here in Ephesus that illustrate this problem?

Ian Fair:

Yes, we are standing right now in the Temple of Domitian. There is a tradition coming from the second century that it was during the closing years of Domitian's reign that the church in Ephesus received the book of Revelation.

Bill Humble:

Back in those days if a Christian refused to say that "Domitian is Lord," he might be put to death. Christians believed that Jesus is Lord — not Caesar — and during the reign of Domitian this confession sometimes brought torture and death.

This temple of Domitian displayed a colossal statue of the emperor exalting him as a deity. Only the head and a forearm, six feet long, have been found. When the Christians at Ephesus read Revelation, they may have been reminded of Domitian and this statue.

Near the center of the city, where the Curetes and Marble streets intersect, archaeologists uncovered a building which some believe was a brothel.

Husnu Ovacik:

I am now sitting in front of this building that is identi-fied as the brothel. It was part of the complex that con-sisted of a bath and public latrine. It was not easy to identify this building as a brothel. But they found this advertisement down the street a few hundred feet. It con-sisted of a lady's head, left foot and a heart. So the mes-sage was clear. If you have a lonely heart, what you are looking for — a lady friend — is on the left ahead.

Bill Humble:

We're not sure about the meaning of this sign on the Marble Street, but who knows, perhaps this is the oldest advertising for the oldest profession.

Ephesus was also the home of the Library of Celsus, one of the greatest libraries in the world.

Library of Celsus at Ephesus.

Husnu Ovacik:
This is a very important mausoleum library. In fact, it was constructed for Celsus who was a proconsul of Rome and a governor here.

Bill Humble:
This library was built by Julius Aquila to honor his father, Celsus, who was a Roman senator and proconsul of Asia. The construction began in 110 A.D. and was finished about twenty years later. This building served a double purpose: it was a library and also a tomb for Celsus.

Husnu Ovacik:
The mausoleum and the sarcophagus of Celsus is in the back under the library. This building functioned as a library till the end of the city.

Bill Humble:
The beautiful restoration work has been done by Austrian archaeologists. But western Turkey has many earthquakes. When we asked an official of the Ephesus Museum about this, he said, "When we have another earthquake, we will have to start the restoration work all over again."

Next to the library, archaeologists found a first-century inscription with the word "lecture hall." This might be a reference to the School of Tyrannus where Paul taught.

Husnu Ovacik:
This library contained over 12,000 scrolls of books in the second century A.D.

Bill Humble:
The Library of Celsus was, in fact, the third greatest library in the ancient world. The other two were at Alexandria and Pergamum. We will visit the one at Pergamum later.

The Marble Street was another major thoroughfare. It ran from the Library of Celsus to the theater. It was paved with marble, as the name suggests, and it was lined with columns and statues.

Major streets in Ephesus leading to the Library of Celsus.

Top: Marble Street.

Right: Curetes Street.

The commercial agora, or market of the city was located along the Marble Street. A large monumental gateway next to the Library of Celsus connected the plaza in front of the library with the agora. The restoration of this impressive gateway is the most recent archaeological work that has been done in Ephesus.

Ian Fair:
We have just come through the monumental gateway at the Library of Celsus into the commercial agora behind me. The agora was where the commerce of an ancient Greek city was carried on. The agora here at Ephesus was the largest and most beautiful anywhere in the world. This agora was a square, 360 feet long on each side. It had a beautiful sundial in the center and columns around the sides.

This is where the people of the city did their shopping. The bakers, potters and tailors had shops in this agora. Here Demetrius and the other silversmiths sold silver images of Artemis to the people who came from all over the world to worship at the Temple of Artemis.

Bill Humble:
The Temple of Artemis, or the Temple of Diana as the Romans knew it, was the glory of Ephesus and one of the seven wonders of the world. But the temple was destroyed so completely that nothing is left today except scattered pieces of marble. Over the centuries several feet of dirt covered the site, and no one remembered where it was. When the British began searching for the temple in the 1860's, it took them six years to find the ruins. They restored one column to mark the site, and that column is home for a family of storks today.

A temple to the mother goddess of Asia was built on this site about 1,000 B.C. It was destroyed by fire in 356 B.C., on the very night Alexander the Great was born. When the Ephesians rebuilt their temple, it was the largest structure anywhere in the world — 361 feet long — and the first building of such size to be built entirely of marble.

Sadly, these fragments don't give us much of an idea of what the temple looked like. But there are two other temples, better preserved, that can help us visualize the magnificence of the Temple of Artemis.

One is the Parthenon in Athens. The Parthenon was built about 100 years before the Temple of Artemis. Architecturally the two temples were very similar, but the temple at Ephesus was four times as large as the Parthenon. The Parthenon has forty-six columns. The Temple of Artemis in Ephesus had 127 columns that were twice as tall. Thirty-six columns had sculptured bases that were overlaid with gold. The British Museum has one of these bases, seven and a half feet in diameter. We can hardly imagine what a row of tall columns like this, overlaid with gold, would have looked like.

The Temple of Apollo at Didyma, sixty miles south of Ephesus, also helps us appreciate the Temple of Artemis. This temple was built at about the same time as the one in Ephesus and was designed by Paionius, one of the architects who worked at Ephesus. It is almost as large as the temple at Ephesus. Two of the massive columns are still standing. Remember that the Temple of Artemis had 127 columns like these. This temple, with 122 columns, was the home of the oracle of Apollo. Kings and generals from everywhere came here to seek counsel.

The Temple of Artemis was destroyed by the Goths in the third century. In the sixth century, Justinian reused some of the columns in Hagia Sophia, his great church in Constantinople. Even though the temple is gone, many images of Artemis have survived. This one was found under the civic agora and is made of alabaster. Artemis was a fertility goddess, and she was always pictured with many symbols of fertility.

This is the great theater in Ephesus and it is the scene of one of the most dramatic moments in Paul's ministry, recorded in Acts 19. This theater was already 300 years old when Paul's enemies stirred up a riot here, but it was enlarged by Emperor Claudius at about the time Paul lived here.

Husnu Ovacik:
The theater of Ephesus was constructed right after Alexander, but what we see here is almost totally a Roman theater. We don't know exactly what the capacity of the Hellenistic theater was, but it now is estimated to have a capacity of 24,000.

Bill Humble:
The theater was built on the side of Mount Pion, and its 24,000 seats were in sixty-six rows up the mountainside. The acoustics are so perfect that when a coin is dropped on the marble stage, the sound can be heard clearly on the topmost row.

Near the end of Paul's three-year ministry at Ephesus, a tumultuous riot rocked this theater. It was incited by Demetrius and the silversmiths who were being hurt by Paul's preaching. The Temple of Artemis was the foundation of the city's prosperity. People came from all over the Roman world to worship Artemis. While here they bought silver shrines. The temple was also a treasury or bank, and silver and gold poured in from many countries.

But Paul's preaching was so effective that the worship of Artemis was in decline. The silversmiths were losing money so they stirred up a riot. The city was in an uproar, and a mob milled around in this theater shouting "Great is Artemis of the Ephesians."

Paul wanted to confront the mob, but his friends would not let him. Later, as Paul looked back on those days, he remembered that he had despaired for his life. He wrote, "We felt the sentence of death" (2 Corinthians 1:8-9). Paul also said that he "fought the wild beasts at Ephesus" (1 Corinthians 15:32). This may refer to Demetrius and his other enemies. It's possible that he actually fought wild animals in the stadium, or maybe even here in this theater.

Ephesus had another major street, the Arcadian Way, and it stretched from the theater to the sea.

Husnu Ovacik:
The Arcadian is actually the harbor street. In other words, at the end of this street was the harbor at the

time of the New Testament. The sea is now seven miles away to the west.

Bill Humble:

Ephesus is located on the Cayster River. Over the centuries the river has filled the harbor with silt. It was already a major problem in the first century. Today, we can't even see the water of the Aegean Sea, but in New Testament times it came to the end of the Arcadian Way and that's where the ships anchored. We can visualize ships tied up at piers, and we can see Paul — and later John — coming down the gangplank and walking into the city on the Arcadian Way.

The first churches had been planted in Asia about forty years before Revelation was written. By the end of the first century Asia had many churches and Christians. But those churches faced serious problems. In most of the seven letters the Lord has praise and encouragement, but these are tempered with rebukes and warnings. Hanging like a sword over all the churches was Rome and her claim that "Caesar is Lord." Ian, what was the Lord's message to Ephesus?

Ian Fair:

The letter to the Ephesians is the first of the seven letters of Jesus to the church in Asia. Perhaps it is first because of the prominence of the church in Ephesus. Jesus begins by commending the church for its hard work, its faithfulness and its doctrinal purity.

But doctrine and works alone, unbalanced by a love and passion for Jesus, would not carry the Ephesians through the trials they would soon have to endure. Jesus' message was simple and direct, "But I have this against you, that you have abandoned the love you had at first. Remember then from what you have fallen, repent and do the works you did at first."

Their reward for faithful loving service to Jesus was that if they should die as conquerors — which is John's favorite term for martyrdom — they would "eat of the tree of life" and live forever.

Bill Humble:

In the Lord's letter to the church here in Ephesus, He warned that unless they repented, He would remove their candlestick out of its place. They must have repented, because the candlestick was not removed — at least not for hundreds of years — and the Christian faith became extremely strong in Asia and in Ephesus.

Let me give you an couple of examples. This is the Arcadian Way that leads from the sea to the great theater. At the fourth, fifth or sixth century there was one of the intersections on the Arcadian Way that had four great columns with a statue atop each column. Those statues were of Matthew, Mark, Luke and John.

Let me give you a second example. In the sixth century the Emperor Justinian built a great church here in Ephesus over the grave of John. We are going to visit that church.

The Church of John was built on a hill about three miles from the city, overlooking the site where the Temple of Artemis then lay in ruins. The church was nearly 400 feet long. It was constructed of red brick and marble and richly decorated with six large domes, many columns and Byzantine crosses.

The Church of John built by Emperor Justinian in the sixth century A.D.

The Ephesus Museum has a scale model, and this gives us a good idea of what Justinian's church looked like.

Extensive restoration work is now being done, and this shows its impressive size and beauty.

Ian Fair:

This baptistry is beautiful. The existence of this baptistry here, as I go down into it, leaves few questions in mind as to the mode of baptism, at least in the sixth century.

Bill Humble:

This is the traditional site of John's grave. We know that he wrote Revelation from Patmos. But according to the church fathers, after Domitian died John was released from exile, came to Ephesus and died here. We do know that in the second century Christians believed that this was John's grave, and four centuries later Justinian built this church over the site.

The church saw many changes between the first century — when Paul and John walked these streets — and the sixth century when Justinian built his church. The time when Christians had to confess that "Caesar is Lord" or face death was a distant memory. Now Christianity was the state religion of the empire, and it was easy to confess that "Jesus is Lord" without cost or commitment. The beast of Revelation was now the patron of the church. As Jesus walked among His lampstands, He might have warned Ephesus, "With all your outward strength and wealth, I see only the inward weakness and decay."

Only a hundred years after Justinian, a new religion — Islam — swept out of Arabia and its armies eventually conquered Asia. The seven churches withered and died. And just the Lord had warned, the lampstand at Ephesus was gone.

3

The Letter to Ephesus

That Jesus would begin His letters to the church in Asia with one to Ephesus is not surprising. Ephesus was the leading city of the Roman province of Asia. There seems little question that the church in Ephesus was one of the great churches of the first century. The church had been established at least as early as Paul's second missionary journey (A.D. 53-58), and most likely considerably earlier.

We first read of Ephesus in Acts 18. In Ephesus, Apollos "spoke and taught accurately the things concerning Jesus, though he knew only the baptism of John." Priscilla and Aquila took Apollos aside and "expounded to him the way of God more accurately." After this, Luke indicates that the brethren in Ephesus wrote the brethren in Achaia encouraging them to receive Apollos when he arrived there.

Paul himself spent at least two years in Ephesus, teaching in the hall of Tyranus (Acts 19:10). A decade or more later Paul left Timothy, his trusted co-worker and evangelist, in Ephesus to continue the tradition of sound teaching Apollos, Priscilla and Aquila, and Paul himself had established there. Finally, in the closing years of his own ministry and of the first century, the aged apostle John ministered to the church in Ephesus. It is possible that the gospel of John was written while John was in Ephesus.

This church had enjoyed some of the great gospel preachers, with a heavy emphasis on sound doctrine. It was to become a leading and pivotal church in Asia and Christendom for more than 500 years.

Theater at Ephesus. Site of riot over Paul's preachings against idols to Artemis (Acts 19).

Jesus begins His letter to Ephesus by identifying Himself in terms of the vision John had seen of Him in Revelation 1:12-16. This vision of Jesus is one of a kingly being, clothed in the magnificent regalia of divinity. The impact of this vision is that Jesus should not be seen as a defeated Messiah, but as a powerful reigning Lord. Jesus holds the seven stars in his right hand, indicating that it is He who controls the eternal destiny of the universe, not Caesar. Jesus is the reigning Lord of the universe. He is also the one who is ever present in the life of the church, walking constantly among the seven churches. No matter what circumstances are to be faced by the church, the church is guaranteed Jesus' abiding presence.

Jesus begins the body of His letter to Ephesus with the statement that He knows all about the church, "I know your works." In fact, He begins each of the seven letters with much the same statement. This is a most sobering, yet encouraging thought. Jesus knows all about every church and every individual Christian. Jesus knows our strengths, our weaknesses, our sufferings and our needs. In the case of Ephesus, He knew that this congregation was a hard working, faithful and enduring church. He knew they were a doctrinally sound church, having been taught from early years by some of the greatest teachers in the church and having tested and rejected those who called themselves apostles, but were in fact false teachers. (See 1 John 4:1, which was most likely written by John while he was in Ephesus.)

The point is that this church was an active, faithful and doctrinally sound congregation, yet there was a major weakness in their spiritual life and witness. They were motivated by the wrong purpose. They lacked the love that had initially motivated them. In the context of the theology and message of Revelation this seems most likely to first be a reference to their love for Jesus and then for one another. Unless this church was driven, controlled and held together by their love for Jesus (2 Corinthians 5:14) they would be unable to withstand the demands to worship the Roman Emperor and the consequent persecutions for refusal to do so.

With telling clarity, G.B. Caird, in his commentary, *The Revelation of Saint John the Divine*, writes, "The one charge against the Ephesians is that their intolerance of imposture, their unflagging loyalty, and their hatred of heresy had bred an inquisitorial spirit which left no room for love. They had set out to be defenders of the faith, arming themselves with the heroic virtues of truth and courage, only to discover that in the battle they had lost the one quality without which all others are worthless ...

John ... recognizes the appalling danger of a religion prompted more by hate than by love."

Jesus warns the Ephesians that unless they refocus and recenter their faith they will lose their right to be a church. He refers to the church as a "lampstand," indicating the role the church plays in the community. Its role should not be defined simply by its hard work and defense of doctrinal purity, but by love — love for Jesus and love for people.

Jesus' warning that He will come to them to remove their lampstand is not a warning of the end-of-the-world judgment, but of His constant "coming" to His church in both judgment and support. It is a reminder of Jesus' constant abiding presence with and in His church.

The reference to the Nicolaitans is a reminder that Jesus will not tolerate immoral practice. Little is known about the Nicolaitans other than they were a licentious, antinomian group who emphasized grace while tolerating moral laxity. Those who love Jesus hate immorality. Doctrinal intensity is not necessarily to be equated with moral faithfulness.

In the letter to the church in Ephesus, Jesus introduces one of the dominant themes of Revelation: Those who conquer. "Conquering" is a significant term in Revelation. John will progressively develop this theme as he moves through the scroll of Revelation 5 and unfolds God's plan for handling the problem of evil and suffering. In the eyes of the world, martyrdom for Jesus was seen as defeat. However, John's message to those Christians facing martyrdom was that death was in reality victory and that the martyr is raised as a conqueror for Jesus. (Revelation 12:11) The message to Ephesus was that those who die as martyrs, thereby conquering Satan, will eat of the tree of life and live forever.

The seriousness of Jesus' warning or exhortation is repeated in each letter with a Jewish or Hebrew idiom:

"He who has an ear, let him hear what the Spirit says to the churches." Jesus' word is a spirit filled warning to the church.

The condition of the church in Ephesus can be summed up in one brief statement: Faithful but lacking; religious but having lost their first love.

The message for the church today is clear. Faithfulness, hard work and doctrinal fidelity are fundamental to the Christian faith but should never become the core of the Christian faith. Christians in today's environment will be identified by their love for Jesus and His purpose, which is to be a servant to our neighbors and a world enslaved in sin. The world will know Christians by their love, not simply because they go to church regularly and defend the faith. However, because of their love for Jesus, Christians will work hard and be faithful to sound doctrine.

Each Christian should examine his or her faith. One should ask himself, "What lies at the center of my faith and practice? What is the confession of my faith? What motivates me and controls me? What gives me courage, hope and stability in my life?"

This letter also reminds us that there is no power other than Jesus in control of this world. It is His world. We are reminded also that without love at the center of our faith and practice we are not His church. This letter to Ephesus challenges us to understand that church faithfulness, hard work, and concern for the sound doctrine are the outgrowth of our love for Jesus and for one another, not the foundation of our faith or the essential criteria for that faith.   **IF**

Questions for Class Discussion

1. Why was the church in Ephesus such a great congregation?

2. What was the nature of the problem in the church in Ephesus?
3. How does a church slip to where it gets its faith off-center, as was the case in Ephesus?
4. What actions can we take to make sure we remain both doctrinally pure and that we show the type of love that Jesus expects?
5. What was the spirit of the Nicolaitans? How or where do we see this tendency today?
6. What can we do today to ensure that we do not become like the church in Ephesus?
7. What did it mean to be a conqueror in Revelation? What is the message in this for us today?

4

Smyrna, Thyatira and Philadelphia

Bill Humble:

Just like many ancient travellers, we left Ephesus, travelled about thirty-five miles north along the Aegean Sea, and we are now in Smyrna. Smyrna was the second of the seven of the seven churches of Asia. In New Testament times it was a large city, estimated population more than a hundred thousand, and a beautiful city. One ancient writer said that it might be the most beautiful city in the world. But unfortunately, much of that ancient magnificence cannot be seen today. The reason is ancient Smyrna now lies buried under one of the largest cities of Turkey.

Izmir is a seaport city with a population of nearly two million. In ancient times Smyrna was guarded by a fort on a hill overlooking the city, and we have a panoramic view of Izmir and the Aegean Sea from this fortress.

If an ancient traveller had been wanting to visit the seven cities of Asia, he would have begun at Ephesus. From Ephesus, the natural route of travel was to follow Roman roads north to Smyrna, then to Pergamum. It's about a hundred miles from Ephesus to Pergamum. The traveller would then have turned southeastward to Thyatira and Sardis, then Philadelphia and Laodicea, a distance of 150 miles. From Laodicea back to Ephesus, and the triangle was complete.

Look at Revelation 2-3 and this is the same order John followed in writing to the seven churches.

We can see from the map that the Aegean Sea was very important to Smyrna and the other churches of Asia.

These cities were first settled by colonists who crossed the Aegean Sea from Greece many centuries before Christ, and they remained Greek cities in language and culture. Ephesus and Smyrna were seaports on the Aegean, and in New Testament times the cities stood on trade routes that connected the Aegean countries with the East.

Husnu Ovacik:

Well, this is Izmir, my home town. I am proud that I was born here because this is also the city of Homer and Polycarp. Unfortunately, I cannot show you so much of the Roman or Hellenistic city of Smyrna because the modern city has grown on the ruins of these historical sites.

Bill Humble:

Archaeologists can't tear down modern buildings to get to the ancient city, so the agora is the only site from New Testament times that can still be seen today.

This is the state agora of Smyrna, where the business of the city was transacted. But this is not the agora that was there in John's day. We know that the city was destroyed by an earthquake, probably in A.D. 177. The emperor at that time was Marcus Aurelius. He knew what a beautiful city Smyrna was. He wept when he heard of its destruction and gave a ten year remission of taxes so that the city could be rebuilt. So everything we see now, the beautiful columns and subterranean vaults, all comes from the late second century.

The state agora in a Greek city was where the governmental affairs were carried on. This agora had a large courtyard — nearly 400 feet long — and was surrounded by columns. Some of the columns are still standing. The stoa around the agora was three stories high. It had the colonnaded portico, which was two stories high, and this was built above a vaulted basement.

Husnu Ovacik:

The northern part of the agora you see behind me, was in the form of a basilica, as you can see from the columns in the middle.

Bill Humble:
Smyrna was truly a beautiful city, as these columns show. The marble beams resting on top of the columns are called the architrave. All the public buildings had beautiful carvings, as we can see from the marble fragments scattered around the site. It's not surprising that Marcus Aurelius called Smyrna "the glory of Asia."

Husnu Ovacik:
Altogether it is one of the biggest agoras that we have preserved in the country.

Columns in the civic agora at Smyrna.

Bill Humble:
Here is a column lying on the ground that is interesting because the fluting was never finished. It shows how the masons did their work. There was a large basement under much of the agora. The basement rooms had vaulted ceilings. The Romans knew how to build arches, and these arches supported the weight of the tall columns of the agora above them. After 2,000 years of earthquakes, the vaulted ceilings are still intact. We can see the skills of the stone masons even in these underground rooms.

Except for this state agora, all the other public buildings of Smyrna lie buried under the modern city. We know that Smyrna had many temples to the Greek gods. The largest was a temple to Zeus that overlooked the Aegean Sea. Smyrna also had a large stadium and a theater that seated 20,000. The city had a statue of its most illustrious son, the poet Homer, who was born here about 800 B.C. But with the modern city covering these ancient buildings, we do not even know where they were [located].

When the Lord wrote to the church here, He warned them that they faced tribulations. One of these was emperor worship. About sixty years before Revelation was written, the Romans decided to choose one city in Asia to be the "temple-keeper" — where the emperor would be worshiped. Several cities competed for the honor, but Smyrna was chosen and built the first temple for the emperor in Asia. Ancient coins have pictures of this temple and one that was built later for Hadrian.

Ian, we know that all the seven churches faced the danger of persecution and the letter to Smyrna talks about tribulation. One of the most famous martyrdoms in early church history happened right here. Tell us about it.

Ian Fair:
This was the martyrdom of Polycarp in about A.D. 155. When Polycarp was brought before the proconsul Quadratus and said, "Eighty and six years have I served him, and he never once wronged me; How then shall I blaspheme my King, Who hath saved me?" (*Fox's Book of Martyrs*, Zondervan Publishing House, Grand Rapids, Michigan, 1967, p. 9). Because of his refusal to worship Caesar, Polycarp and others were martyred here in Smyrna.

Polycarp was burned at the stake in the stadium — it was a public spectacle — but his trial before Quadratus may have been held here in the agora.

Polycarp had been a student of the apostle John. When he died in the flames, one of the last of John's disciples was gone.

Bill Humble:
A remarkable part of this is the role played by the Jews. The records say that they helped to bring the wood to build the fire, even though it was the Sabbath day when it happened.

Ian Fair:
The Lord's letter to Smyrna shows the hostility between the Christians and the Jews. Jesus said, "I know ... the slander of those who say they are Jews and are not, but are a synagogue of Satan." So I guess it's not surprising that the Jews would help burn Polycarp to death.

Bill Humble:
It's hard to walk around this agora without thinking of Polycarp and the other Christians who died for their faith. The marble lion is a reminder that believers died in many ways. Sometimes they were thrown into the arena to fight the wild beasts.

The Christians who faced these dangers needed strength and encouragement, and they found it in the Lord's letter. It is the shortest of the seven letters and it has only praise and comfort. No rebukes.

Ian Fair:
The letter to Smyrna is the second letter of John to the seven churches of Asia. It is one of two letters that is positive and has no negative condemnation of the church. The other one is to Philadelphia. This is a beautiful little letter. It's very short and indicates that the church is going to go through a very severe period of testing, persecution and suffering. But it encourages the church — if you are faithful unto death you will receive the crown of life. If you are willing to die for Jesus, you will live and reign with Jesus.

The message for Smyrna is that faithfulness to Jesus is more powerful than even the reality of suffering and death. Our victory is guaranteed by the resurrection of Jesus and our faithfulness to Him, even in the face of death.

There is another message. The Christians in Smyrna were poor. Jesus said, I know [of] your poverty — yet you are rich. Whenever the church is poor in spirit — as Jesus said in one of the beatitudes — when it knows its need for God, then it is rich like Smyrna.

Bill Humble:

We have now arrived at Thyatira, an inland town about sixty miles northeast of Smyrna. I remember that one of Paul's first converts on the continent of Europe was Lydia, a seller of purple from Thyatira. Our visit here may be a little disappointing because there is not much to be seen of that ancient New Testament city — even less than at Smyrna. The reason is the same. This town lies buried under the modern Turkish town of Akhisar.

One small area, right in the middle of Akhisar, has been excavated. The archaeologists found the ruins of only two interesting buildings: a temple of Apollo and a church built in honor of John.

Husnu Ovacik:

These ruins [around us] are from the Temple of Apollo. Now Apollo was worshiped here for a long time, but we don't know what the temple was like because on this site many buildings were later constructed. Also, the Church of St. John was constructed here in the sixth century A.D.

Bill Humble:

None of the walls or columns of the Temple of Apollo are still standing. But many column drums and marble fragments are scattered around, and these show that it was an important temple. The archaeologists found arches that had fallen, but instead of restoring them, they have laid them out on the ground.

Here is a row of column bases that are still in place on the stylobate. Stylobate is an archaeological term, and it refers to the massive blocks of cut stone that were laid end to end as a foundation for a row of columns.

The god Apollo was worshiped in many cities. His most famous temple was at Delphi in Greece, and people came from all over the world to ask the oracle's advice. The oracle also spoke at the great temple in Didyma, south of Ephesus, that we have already visited.

Husnu Ovacik:

Apollo is the sun god. Being the sun god, nothing is a secret from him because he can see everything from above. He is responsible for the oracles. He is [also] responsible for the medical treatment of everybody.

Bill Humble:

Along with the Temple of Apollo, the archaeologists have found an ancient church. It was built in the sixth century in honor of John. The walls, constructed of brick and stone, are still standing. As we walk around the nave, we can see that this was an impressive church building — not as large as Justinian's church at Ephesus, but still impressive for a smaller town like Thyatira.

Arched doorways led from the main part of the church into rooms along the side. This church, like others that we see in the seven cities of Asia, was built about 200 years after the Roman persecutions had ended. They show that the Christian faith was very strong in Asia up to the time the Muslims came in the seventh century.

The New Testament has only two references to Thyatira: [As] the home of Lydia in Acts 16, and in the letter here in Revelation. However, we have other historical sources about the city. We know that trade guilds were important in Thyatira. These guilds gave the city its prosperity. Inscriptions show that there were guilds of bakers, potters, wool-merchants, dyers, brass workers, and even slave-traders. The city was famous for dying purple cloth. This may explain why Lydia, who came from Thyatira, was a seller of purple at Philippi.

When Jesus wrote to Thyatira, He described Himself as the one whose feet were like burnished bronze. The Greek word for "burnished bronze" has never been found anywhere else, and it may have been the trade-name for the metal workers guild in Thyatira.

The trade guilds posed some hard choices for the Christians who lived there. If a Christian was going to work in a guild, he might be forced to go along with the guild's activities, including the immoral fertility rites and the pagan sacrifices. But if the Christian refused to go along, he might be without a job.

As the church faced this problem, one party argued for compromise. They taught that even though Jesus was their Lord, it would still be all right to share in the pagan sacrifices. This party was led by a woman called Jezebel, and she is condemned in the strongest language in Revelation.

Thyatira was the least important of the seven cities of Asia, but the letter to the church here was the longest of the seven. Why did Jesus have so much to say to this church?

Ian Fair:

The letter to Thyatira is interesting because it has a mixed message. Jesus begins by praising the church and commending the church for their love, their faith, their service, their patient endurance, and the fact that their later works were better than their first works. But then He turns and condemns them because they tolerated a Jezebel-type woman.

The central problem in Revelation was one of compromising one's faith. In this letter to Thyatira, Jesus condemns the church there for tolerating a Jezebel-type woman who taught the church to compromise their faith by committing adultery and eating food offered to idols.

Christians today can learn much from this church. The church of Jesus cannot afford to compromise its faith with a secular mind and sensual immorality. Jesus tells us that His eyes are like a flaming fire. He can see through our insincerity and the spiritual veneer that we sometimes hide behind. When we are tempted to go along with our immoral culture, we must renew our faith in the Lord and His moral standards. If we vacillate and compromise, then we deny Him.

Philadelphia was about eighty miles east of Smyrna. It was located in a wide valley where the volcanic soil was very fertile. Today, the finest grapes in Turkey are grown in this region. Philadelphia was the youngest of the seven cities of Asia. King Attalus of Pergamum built the city about 150 B.C. Attalus was so devoted to one of his brothers that he was given the title *Philadelphus*, the one who loves his brother. That title became the name of his new city.

Like Smyrna and Thyatira, Philadelphia is buried under a modern city. As a result, there are fewer antiquities here at Philadelphia than any of the other churches. There's an ancient church honoring John, but that's all. Everything else, including a stadium and theater, are somewhere under the modern buildings of Alashehir.

The church of John was built around A.D. 600. Archaeologists are currently doing a little work around the church. They have found some of the foundations and walls of earlier buildings that stood on this site before the church was built, but they have not learned what these earlier buildings were.

Archaeologists work in squares — usually five meters on a side — and here is a square near the wall of John's church. They have found a piece of marble in the wall of the square, and it's still there. A column with unusual spiral fluting lies on the bottom of the square. Here and there, fragments of carved marble give us a glimpse of Philadelphia's beauty. The massive walls and arches of the Church of St. John that are still standing show that it was a very large building, much larger than the church at Thyatira.

We have now visited four of the seven cities of Asia, and three of these have had Byzantine churches built in honor of John: Justinian's great church in Ephesus, then Thyatira, and now Philadelphia. It may seem a little strange that all these churches honored John and not Paul. While Paul was at Ephesus, his converts had planted many of these churches. But centuries later when the churches were free to erect buildings, it was John they chose to honor. John had lived at Ephesus and was buried there. As an old man, he had admonished the church to love one another. And Jesus had chosen John, on Patmos, to "write what you see in a book and send it to the seven churches." So the churches remembered and honored John.

Judging from the Lord's letter to Philadelphia, this must have been the very best of the seven churches, for Jesus had only praise for them — not a word of rebuke. The church here had kept His word, they had not denied His name, and they had endured patiently. Because of their faithfulness, Jesus had set before them an "open door" of opportunity for evangelizing and witnessing for Him. And because they had kept His word, He promised to keep them from the hour of trial ahead. There were other promises. They would be a pillar in the temple of God and they would wear the Lord's own new name.

Let's compare these beautiful promises with the Lord's threat to the church in Ephesus. He warned them that unless they repented, he would remove their lampstand out of its place. It took several centuries for this to happen, but when the armies of Islam swept across Asia, Ephesus and the other cities fell and the Christian faith withered and died.

But not in Philadelphia. This city was the last bastion of the Christian faith in Asia. Long after the other cities fell, Philadelphia remained a free Christian city in the midst of a Muslim world. The church was still enjoying the Lord's promises.

But finally, Philadelphia fell in 1391. And today in Asia, where the church was once stronger than anywhere else in the world, the churches lie in ruins and the minarets are everywhere. Sadly, all of the seven lampstands are gone.

5

The Letter to Smyrna

The terms used by Jesus in introducing Himself to the church in Smyrna are again drawn from John's description of Jesus as the divine, reigning Lord of the universe (Revelation 1:12-16). He is "the first and the last," indicating His divine character. He is the one who died on the cross but who lives forevermore through His powerful resurrection (Revelation 1:17-18). These would be encouraging words for those who — like Jesus their Lord — would shortly be faced with martyrdom for their faith in God and Jesus.

The theology of Revelation develops the point that just as Jesus was obedient even unto death on the cross, so His disciples would need to take up their cross daily and follow Him — even if it meant physical death (Luke 9:23ff). Martyrdom was a daily encounter for disciples in the first century, so much so that Paul and Peter clearly identify discipleship with suffering, persecution and martyrdom (Acts 14:22; 1 Thessalonians 2:14-16; 3:2-4; 2 Timothy 3:12; 1 Peter 2:19-25; 3:14-18; 4:16; 5:7-10).

But the message continues. God had been faithful to Jesus and had raised Him from death to victory and a crown. So too would God, through Jesus and His Holy Spirit, raise the disciples to victory and a crown (Romans 8:11).

This message of victory over death through martyrdom would have specific meaning for this church in Smyrna, for they would soon have to choose faithfulness to Jesus over death. Jesus knows of their tribulation. He knows of their persecution and slander by the Jews in Smyrna. The Jews thought they were the people of God, but Jesus called them a "synagogue of Satan." The Jews in Smyrna had instigated violent hostility in the community against the Christians, most likely leading to a condition of extreme hardship and poverty. Similar violent Jewish opposition to Christians was also experienced in Philadelphia (Revelation 3:9).

Jesus encourages the disciples in Smyrna not to lose heart, although they would encounter severe persecution and testing for "10 days." Ten days is synonymous with a short period of testing (Daniel 1:12). For their faithfulness unto death, the disciples would be rewarded by God with the "crown of life." In Revelation the term "crown" is the Greek word *stephanos*, meaning a victory laurel like that given in athletic games. In both the letter to Ephesus and Smyrna, the first two letters to the churches in Asia, the reward for dying as a martyr is said to be eternal life. Jesus does not guarantee Christians immunity from suffering and death, but He does promise them eternal life and victory for their martyrdom. They may not escape death in this life, but they need have no fear of the second death or final judgment (Revelation 20:14; 21:8).

In a similar vein, Jesus does not promise us freedom from suffering, hostility or persecution. He does promise us His never failing love and an ultimate victory over death (1 Corinthians 15:51-56).

Perhaps the most encouraging passage in the New Testament is Romans 8:35-39:

> Who shall separate us from the love of Christ?
> Shall tribulation, or distress, or persecution, or

famine, or nakedness, or peril, or sword? As it is written, 'For thy sake we are being killed all the day long; we are regarded as sheep to be slaughtered.' No, in all these things we are more than conquerors through him who loved us. For I am sure that neither death, nor life, nor angels, nor principalities, nor things present, nor things to come, nor powers, nor height, nor depth, nor anything else in all creation, will be able to separate us from the love of God in Christ Jesus our Lord.

One brief sentence summarizes the condition of the church in Smyrna: "Faithful unto death." This message of Jesus to Smyrna would touch history in a poignant and very real manner some 60-70 years later. On this occasion, Polycarp, bishop of Smyrna, was arrested and tried for his faith in Jesus and refusal to worship Caesar as Lord. When confronted by Governor Statius Quadratus, who sympathetically tried to find an opportunity for Polycarp to escape the cruel death that awaited him, Polycarp responded with these touching words, "Eighty and six years have I served him, and he never once wronged me; How then shall I blaspheme my King, Who hath saved me?" (*Fox's Book of Martyrs*, Zondervan Publishing House, Grand Rapids, Michigan, 1967, p. 9). "Faithful unto death." Polycarp went to his death confident in the constant abiding love of Jesus and Jesus' promise that he need have no fear of either the first or the second death.

The letter to Smyrna reminds us that Christians will all too often be faced with periods of testing. Living in a world in which evil is ever present, Christians must be alert to the temptation to compromise their faith and to take the path of least resistance. Polycarp could have compromised his faith and survived his trial, but he knew that such would ultimately lead to the defeat of all that Jesus had died for — namely, his salvation. Polycarp's faith has been for centuries a living testimony of love for Jesus and commitment to principle. **IF**

Questions for Class Discussion

1. In what way does the situation of the Christians in Smyrna have parallels in contemporary society and church life?
2. How does the secular community oppose Christianity today?
3. How should Christians respond to persecution?
4. What might be some modern parallels to the "synagogue of Satan"?
5. How do Jesus' promises help you deal with temptations and trials?
6. Share some stories about Christians whose lives and examples in the face of adversities have made a positive impression on your life.
7. Discuss some conditions in which your personal example and unwillingness to compromise your faith could make a positive contribution to someone else's faith.

6

Che Letter to Chyatira

The introduction of the letter to Thyatira is similar to Jesus' introductions to the other six letters, being drawn from John's initial vision and description of Jesus robed in divine regalia: "The words of the Son of God, who has eyes like a flame of fire, and whose feet are like burnished bronze" (Revelation 2:18). The theological background behind this imagery is difficult to determine. The mention of fire and feet of burnished bronze are reminiscent of Ezekiel's vision of the four living creatures whose responsibility was to maintain and defend the holiness of God. There may be some reference to Micah 4:13, where the feet of bronze are a reference to judging the nations. If this is the case, then Jesus is the one who maintains God's holiness and judges those who oppose God and His people. These themes fit well with the theology of Revelation.

The title "Son of God" opens the way for John's development of a major theme in Revelation drawing from Psalm 2. Psalm 2 became a significant endorsement of Jesus' Messianic role as God's favored Son. Those who die with Jesus in martyrdom will also reign with Him in His kingly realm. They, too, would rule with a "rod of iron" (Revelation 2:27; 12:5; 19:15) — as Jesus rules in fulfillment of Psalm 2.

The sociological background to Jesus' introductory statement is equally fascinating. Thyatira was a thriving

Temple of Apollo at Thyatira.

commercial center with many skilled trade guilds. It was famous for its smelting works, purple dye and cloth works. This was a city without military significance which gained its importance purely from its trade and manufacturing skill.

Jesus acknowledges their "love and faith and service and patient endurance" and that their works had continued to mature. Nevertheless there was a tendency to compromise with immorality. The reference to a Jezebel-like woman (1 Kings 16:31; 2 Kings 9:22) implies immorality and the worst kind of idolatrous opposition to God. Jesus' judgmental language of this type of compromise is as severe as one can read in Scripture, implying Jesus' absolute rejection of those who are seduced by this practice. This compromise cannot be hidden from Jesus who "searches mind and heart" and sees all.

There were some who boasted of knowing "the deep things of Satan." The context obviously relates to the practice of immorality. Christians are encouraged not to be misled into learning these deep things. They are to hold fast to their faith. Those who keep Jesus' works to the end will be rewarded by reigning with Jesus in His kingdom just as He reigns (Revelation 2:27; 20:4ff). This is the major theme of Revelation.

The final statement "I will give him [the conqueror or martyr] the morning star" draws on a collage of Old Testament and Apocryphal references with Messianic overtones. By the time Jesus addressed this letter to the church in Thyatira, the expression "bright and morning star" had become a reference to Jesus' Messianic glory. The conqueror would share in Jesus' Messianic glory.

The church in Thyatira could be described as faithful, loving and maturing, yet plagued by those who see in compromise with immorality a deepened spiritual understanding. It is almost as though this attitude is the forerunner of the modern expression "If you haven't tried it, don't knock it!" Jesus says that there is no need to try what He has already declared to be wrong. **IF**

Questions for Class Discussion

1. This letter begins with imagery of God's holiness. Discuss the meaning of God's holiness.
2. In what ways do the good qualities of the church in Thyatira differ from those of Ephesus (Revelation 2:2)?
3. How can a congregation's works mature (v.19)?
4. What might some of the "deep things of Satan" refer to in our society today?
5. We may not be called on to die as martyrs, but how would the message of Thyatira apply to us today?
6. How was the church of Thyatira similar to the church in Corinth? (See 1 Corinthians 5:1-2 and Revelation 2:20.)
7. "Bright and morning star" described Jesus' Messianic glory. Identify some modern phrases that could describe His glory.

7

The Letter to Philadelphia

Philadelphia was located on the main Roman road between Sardis and Laodicea. Spiritually, the church in Philadelphia was vastly different from its sister congregations in the neighboring cities. Sardis was dead and Laodicea was lukewarm. In sharp contrast, the Lord had only praise for Philadelphia — not a word of rebuke. The church had kept the Lord's word, had not denied His name, and had endured patiently. No other church heard such a gracious "well done" from their Lord.

The Lord's self-identification to Philadelphia is different. Jesus began the first five letters in Revelation 2-3 by saying, "I am ... ." He then described Himself using imagery drawn from the vision in Revelation 1, always with a sense of judgment. But the Lord began the letter to Philadelphia by saying, "The words of the holy one, the true one, who has the key of David, who opens and no one shall shut, who shuts and no one opens" (Revelation 3:7). Holiness and truth are attributes of God, so Jesus is reminding Philadelphia that the one they trust is God. The "key of David" is a reference from Isaiah 22:20-25. During the reign of King Hezekiah (700 B.C.), Eliakim was given the key of David — a symbol of authority. Today, Jesus has the key and sits on David's throne.

The church in Philadelphia had an open door that no one could shut. This probably refers to unique opportunities for evangelism. The British archaeologist, Sir William Ramsay, in his book *Letters to the Seven Churches* (Westminster Press, Philadelphia, 1957, pp. 94-99) noted some interesting parallels between the church in Philadelphia and the city where it was situated. One of these parallels involved outreach of the city and the church. Philadelphia was the youngest of the seven cities of Asia. It had been planted by King Attalus II of Pergamum about 150 B.C. to spread Greek influences into the heartland of Asia Minor. This was so successful that the people of that region, the Lydians, gradually stopped using their own native tongue and began speaking Greek.

Just as the city had been open to cultural changes, the church there had an open door for preaching the Gospel. This opportunity for outreach was there despite the fact that the church, unlike rich Laodicea, had little power. This should warn us that effective evangelism and church growth do not depend on a congregation's wealth, influence or prominence in the community, but on its total dependence on the Lord and His Word.

This letter, like the one to Smyrna, reflects a bitter hostility between the Christians and their Jewish neighbors. Jesus declares that the people who call themselves Jews are not. The ultimate meaning of Jesus' incarnation, death and resurrection is that the true Jew is no longer the fleshly descendant of Abraham but the believer, of any race, who accepts Jesus as God's Son. Since the Jews in Smyrna and Philadelphia had not come to this faith, they were now "a synagogue of Satan" — strong language indeed.

The Lord promised the church, "I will make them come and bow down before your feet, and learn that I have loved you" (Revelation 3:9). What does this mean? That the Jewish community at Philadelphia would become believers? Perhaps so. Many commentators understand the passage this way. It may refer to that dramatic time when every knee will bow "and every tongue confess that Jesus Christ is Lord, to the glory of God the Father" (Philippians 2:10-11).

Notice the play on the word "keep" in Revelation 3:10: "Because you have kept my word of patient endurance, I will keep you from the hour of trial which is coming on the whole world, to try those who dwell upon the earth." The Lord promises to keep those who have kept His word. What a glorious promise!

Wall of the Church of John at Philadelphia.

What was the trial that would come upon the whole earth? Since emperor worship hung like a sword over all the Asian Christians, we might assume that the hour of trial was impending persecution. It was certainly true that emperor worship would be a trial to the Philadelphia Christians. We know that when Polycarp was burned to death at Smyrna, Christians from Philadelphia died in the flames with him. We know, too, that Jews helped gather wood for the fires even though it was the Sabbath, evidence of the hostility seen in this letter.

However, the trial here was probably not the persecution of the church, but rather the Lord's judgment on the church's enemies. The message of Revelation is that even though the believers suffer for a time, ultimately the Lord will pour out His wrath on the beast (Rome) that was tormenting His people. The trial in 3:10 will test "those who dwell upon the earth." This expression usually refers to the unbelievers who oppose the church (Revelation 6:10; 11:10; 13:8,14). Thus, the Lord's promise is that since Philadelphia had endured with patience, He would keep them from the judgment that would finally engulf their enemies.

The promise, "I am coming soon," cannot refer to the Second Coming. Jesus Himself taught that only the Father knows when that day will be (Matthew 24:36), and Revelation pictures a succession of events that must unfold before Jesus returns. So this is probably a promise of the Lord's spiritual presence with His people — as in the Great Commission, "Lo, I am with you always" (Matthew 28:20).

The letter closes with a series of promises to those who conquer. They will be a pillar in the temple of God. This probably refers to heaven. A pillar symbolizes strength and permanence. Once again, Sir William Ramsay has suggested a parallel between the city's history and this promise. Philadelphia had been devastated by an earthquake in A.D. 17. Severe aftershocks continued for years. When the historian Strabo visited there in A.D. 20, he reported that many of the city's inhabitants were still living in huts outside the city, afraid to return to their homes. With such memories, the picture of a pillar in heaven would be most comforting.

The Lord also promises that upon those who conquer He will write the name of God, the name of the New Jerusalem, and His own new name (Revelation 3:12). As Revelation reaches its climax, Jesus "the Faithful and

True" rides on a white horse and wears the name "King of kings and Lord of lords" (Revelation 19:16). To wear this name is to belong to Jesus and to share triumphantly in His kingdom.

Judged by worldly standards, the church in Philadelphia probably had a membership drawn from the underprivileged with little power and strong enemies. It would have been tempting to choose Laodicea, rather than Philadelphia, as a church home. But the Lord has different standards. Judging from His letters, Philadelphia must have been the very best of the seven churches. **BH**

Questions for Class Discussion

1. The "key of David" was an ancient symbol of authority. What modern day images could we use to describe Jesus' authority?
2. What are some of the parallels between the church in Philadelphia and the city where it was located?
3. Do you think the church you attend has open doors like Philadelphia? If so, where are those open doors? How can the church take advantage of them?
4. Who are God's chosen people today?
5. Can you identify any modern parallels to the Jewish opposition to Christians?
6. How can opposition make you stronger and success make you weaker?
7. What did Jesus mean when he said, "I am coming soon."

8

PERGAMUM

Bill Humble:

Jesus once said that a city set on a hill cannot be hidden, and ancient Pergamum was just such a city. It's the third of the seven churches of Asia, and it's about a hundred miles north of Ephesus. The library and temples of Pergamum were located on this hill, the acropolis, that towers nearly a thousand feet above the rest of the city. Sir William Ramsay, one of the earliest English archaeologists who worked here, said that of all the cities of Asia Minor this [one] deserves to be called a royal city because of this spectacular acropolis.

A sacred way goes from the base of the acropolis to the Temple of Asklepios, a half-mile away. From this column-lined street we can see how the acropolis towers over the surrounding plains. We can see the ancient temples and theater on the summit of the acropolis. In New Testament times, the lower city — where many of the common people had their homes — was in the fertile Caicus River valley around the base of the acropolis. Today, that's where the modern city of Bergama is located.

Pergamum had been an important city for many centuries before the birth of Christ. But in the second century B.C., King Attalus began to fear the growing power of Rome to the West. He realized that his kingdom could not hold off the Roman legions. He decided that it would be better to surrender his kingdom to the Romans, rather than wait to be conquered. This happened in 133 B.C. King Attalus made a wise decision, because the Romans rewarded Pergamum in many ways. It was the capital of Asia for the next 250 years and became the center of emperor worship in Asia. For Pergamum, this meant peace and prosperity. But for the Christians who lived here, it meant hard choice and suffering.

Now, let's visit some of the buildings on this imposing acropolis. Just a few years after John wrote Revelation, the people of Pergamum built a great temple in honor of the Emperor Trajan. This temple is the most beautiful building still standing on the acropolis, and we will come back to it later.

Two other buildings, standing side-by-side, were the Temple of Athena and the library. These rows of columns mark the location of the Temple of Athena. Athena was one of the most important Greek goddesses, and the temple here was two stories high with many columns. Although Athena was worshiped here, it was also a museum — perhaps the first museum anywhere.

The library was next to the temple, and the only access to the library was through the temple. The walls of the library that are still standing are not very impressive, and they don't reflect the importance of this library.

Ian, I like libraries. We're sitting together in front of the library here in Pergamum that was the second greatest library in the ancient world. Only Alexandria surpassed it. Tell me about the rivalry between these two libraries.

Ian Fair:

Yes, this is an interesting story. When the King of Pergamum wanted to build a library that would rival that in Alexandria, he hired the librarian from Alexandria. This infuriated the Pharaoh, who put the librarian in prison. The Pharaoh then refused to sell writing material, which was papyrus, to the King of Pergamum. So the King of Pergamum put out a challenge to his people to develop an alternate writing material, and they came up with parchment — which is the use of animal skins for writing material. This is known in Latin as "Pergamum sheets."

Sacred Way from the acropolis to the Temple of Aesklepios.

Bill Humble:
Isn't it true that our greatest biblical manuscripts were written on parchment?

Ian Fair:
Yes, and that also introduced the form that we know as a book — which we call a codex — no longer written on scrolls, but now written on pages in the form of a book.

Bill Humble:
And all that happened right here?

Ian Fair:
Yes, right here in this library.

Bill Humble:
Even though little remains now, this library was more important than the library of Celsus at Ephesus in New Testament days. It gave us parchment, and without that durable writing material we might not have such old trustworthy manuscripts of our New Testament.

Husnu, tell me what finally happened to this library.

Husnu Ovacik:
According to George Bean, it was given as a present by

Antonius — who did not own the library — to Cleopatra, who had other things to do than read.

Bill Humble:
This was the Cleopatra, Queen of Egypt, and the library declined after that?

Husnu Ovacik:
Yes. After several wars, it was burned down and we have nothing left from the library now.

Bill Humble:
But according to Plutarch, this library had 200,000 volumes at the time Mark Antony gave it to Cleopatra.

Ancient cities had to have walls to protect them from threatening armies, and the walls here at Pergamum were built around the top of the acropolis. No enemy could storm these massive walls on the mountaintop, so whenever the city was in danger, the people took refuge inside these walls and were safe.

The Pergamum theater was located on the steep mountainside just below the summit of the acropolis. Music and drama were very important in Greece. Since the cities of Asia were really Greek in language and culture, their theaters were important in preserving their cultural heritage.

But there was no other theater like this one at Pergamum. Every seat had a breath-taking view of the river valley and plain, nearly a thousand feet below. The *cavea*, or seating area, followed the natural contour of the acropolis rock — so this theater was taller and steeper than any other.

Husnu, I know that every one of the seven cities of Asia had its Greek-style theater. But this one at Pergamum is just absolutely spectacular. Tell me how it is different from the other cities.

Husnu Ovacik:
It is not a perfect semicircle. It is less than a semicircle, and in order to compensate for the capacity they have constructed more rows of seats than the regular [theater]. This theater has eighty rows of seats, with a seat-

ing capacity of 10,000. Also, as you can see, it is the steepest *cavea*.

Bill Humble:

The steepest one anywhere. I can just imagine how spectacular it would be to attend a musical concert here at night, listening to the music, and watching the sun set beyond the mountains to the west.

The theater at Pergamum was the steepest anywhere in the Roman world.

Just above the theater, we can see the foundations of the royal balcony, where the king and his guests had their seats. It's a long way from the royal balcony down to the stage. And the stage area was so narrow that they could not build a permanent state building like most Greek theaters have. What is this little temple over here?

Husnu Ovacik:
It was a temple dedicated to Dionysus and constructed in the second century B.C. Then in the third century A.D. it was reconstructed and dedicated to Emperor Caracalla for emperor worship.

Bill Humble:
Emperor worship in the third century?

Husnu Ovacik:
Yes.

Bill Humble:
Caracalla lived more than a hundred years after John wrote Revelation. So this temple shows that for nearly 300 years Pergamum continued to be the main center of emperor worship in Asia.

Pergamum got its water from springs several miles away. They built an aqueduct to bring the water into the city. Long sections of this aqueduct are still in place, and we can see some of them from the acropolis. When they built this aqueduct, they knew enough about hydraulic engineering that they were able to force the water through pipes for the last two miles and then up to the top of the acropolis. So all the palaces and temples up here had plenty of running water.

Now, we're going to leave the acropolis and go down to the lower city, where we can visit the Temple of Asklepios. A sacred way leads from the base of the acropolis to the temple. It's a beautiful street, a half-mile long, paved with marble and lined with columns.

In the Lord's letter to Pergamum, He referred to their city as the place where Satan had his throne and the place where Satan dwells. Where was Satan's throne here in Pergamum? Evidently it was some place of immorality and pagan worship so notorious that the early Christians would have known instantly where it was. But we can't be sure. Where was Satan's throne? There are a number of possibilities. The first one is the Temple of Asklepios where we are now.

This temple, called the Asklepeion, served two functions:

It was a temple where the god was worshiped, and it was also a hospital.

Husnu Ovacik:
   The Asklepeion is very important because it was one of the two biggest hospitals in the ancient world. Also, the doctor Galen was born here and he was trained here. He was trained by healing the injuries of the gladiators from the gladiator school nearby. He is known to be the first doctor who used diagnosis in therapy.

Bill Humble:
   Galen learned anatomy by working on the broken bodies of gladiators. Later, he served as the personal physician for three emperors. One was Caracalla, whose temple we visited on the acropolis.

   In the ancient world medicine and the worship of Asklepios went hand-in-hand. Asklepios was the god of healing, so his temple was the hospital and his priests were the doctors. The greatest temple to Asklepios was at Epidarus in Greece. The one here at Pergamum was begun about 350 B.C., and it became the second greatest in the Roman world. These two temples would have been the "Mayo Clinic" of the ancient world. Sick people came from everywhere to beseech the god for healing.

   The Asklepeion was a square area, about 400 feet long, with colonnaded stoas on three sides. Several of the large columns are still standing with the architrave — the marble beams across the top — still in place. The temple had a small theater seating about 3,500. It's been restored and is now used for musical concerts.

   Every sanctuary of Asklepios was built around a sacred spring where the water was believed to have healing powers. Some of the springs here are still flowing. Along with medicines, the priests used a variety of treatments: bathing in pools like this, mud-packs, and blood-letting.

   They also used the rite of incubation. A second-century scholar names Aristides, who was chronically ill, came to Pergamum for healing. He has described the rite of incubation. The patient spent the night alone in an underground room. In the words of Aristides, "They slept the night in the temple, in hopes that the god Asklepios would either miraculously cure their ailment or appear to them in a dream with a prescription to cure it."

The patient may have waited in underground rooms that have not been excavated, or perhaps in this long underground hallway. Notice the openings in the ceiling. If a priest came during the night and spoke through the opening and told the sick man he would be healed, and if he believed it was the voice of Asklepios himself, it might well bring healing — psycho-therapy at an ancient hospital.

But let's go back to Satan's throne. How could anyone think that a place of healing could be an evil place where Satan dwells? The answer is simple. The serpent was the symbol of Asklepios. Wherever Asklepios was worshiped, there were pictures of snakes. Some were crude, others beautifully carved on marble columns. And even today, the snake remains the symbol of the medical profession.

But for Christians, the serpent was Satan who had tempted Adam and Eve and brought sin and death into the world. So for Christians, the Asklepeion might have been where Satan had his throne.

But there are at least two other places in Pergamum where Satan might have had his throne. Since the Asklepeion was a place of healing and service, one of the other places may be more likely.

Where was Satan's throne? A second possibility is that it may have been the great altar of Zeus located on the platform behind me. Many scholars believe this is the right answer. The area was excavated by the Germans in the 1870's, and they planted the trees to mark the spot.

The Altar of Zeus was built about 160 B.C. to commemorate the victory of Pergamum in driving back the Gauls who were invading from the North. It was situated on a natural terrace about eighty feet below the summit of the acropolis and could be seen from far away. Near the altar an agora served the needs of the people who came to the upper city. Some of the massive walls near the agora are still in place.

When the Germans began work here in the 1870's, they quickly discovered that the altar was in ruins. Hundreds of years earlier, sections had been knocked down and reused in building fortifications. The archaeologists recovered all the fragments they could find, took them to Berlin, and spent many years restoring the altar. It was finally put on display in 1930.

The word "altar" may be misleading. The altar was a large building, shaped like a horseshoe around marble steps that led up to the altar where Zeus was worshiped. This building was about fifty feet high with delicate Ionic columns around the top.

The altar has a frieze carved in marble around the base. The frieze is 360 feet long and it has more than a hundred larger-than-life size figures. The figures are the Olympian gods and goddesses fighting the giants from Gaul. Here the gods of the sea are driving the giants up the steps.

Athena holds one of the giants by the hair, and a sacred serpent is about to strike him to death. You can see the fear of death on his face.

Nyx, the goddess of night, is about to throw a vase at a giant. The vase had a deadly snake coiled around it.

This altar is one of the greatest treasures of Hellenistic art, and Turkey would like to have it back. We saw posters at archaeological sites in Turkey with the plea, "We want it back." But it is not likely that the Germans will ever return it.

The altar honored Zeus and Athena Nike, the goddess of victory, but the frieze included most of the Greek pantheon. Zeus was often called "Zeus the Savior," and all of this would have been so anathema to the Christians that the Altar of Zeus might have been Satan's throne.

But there is one more possibility.

Where was Satan's throne? A third possibility is that the expression refers to a series of temples dedicated to emperor worship. The most spectacular of these is the Temple of Trajan that was built about twenty years after John wrote Revelation. All of these temples posed a tremendous problem to Christians when they were forced to confess, "Caesar is Lord" — or face death.

This temple was built by Hadrian, Trajan's adopted son, who followed his father on the throne in A.D. 117. A new festival honoring Zeus and Trajan was begun in this temple. Later, Hadrian was also worshiped here. The temple is over 200 feet long and stands on the highest point on the acropolis. The columns that are still standing, with part of the pediment restored, show that this was a temple of surpassing beauty.

Ian, how early did they begin practicing emperor worship here in Pergamum?

Ian Fair:

Pergamum had been the main center for emperor worship in Asia for 150 years before they built this temple to Trajan. The Romans allowed Pergamum to build a temple to Augustus in 29 B.C., the first one in Asia. For the next forty years this was the only place in Asia where the emperor was worshiped. Later, when temples were built at Smyrna and Ephesus, the one at Pergamum remained the most important.

Archaeologists have not found the Temple of Augustus. They have found coins with a picture of the temple on one side, and this temple of Trajan on the other side. Also, we need to remember the temple dedicated to Caracalla near the theater. So Pergamum was "thrice temple-keeper" for the emperors: first Augustus, then Trajan and Caracalla.

Bill Humble:

We also need to remember that Pergamum had many other pagan temples: the Altar of Zeus and temples to Athena, Asklepios, and many others. Paul would have called it a city filled with idolatry. For Christians, the temples to Zeus and the other Greek gods were no big problem. They could be ignored.

But not the emperor's temple. The Christians in the seven churches sometimes faced a cruel test — burn a little incense before the emperor's statue and confess that "Caesar is Lord" or face the charge of treason. Christ or

Caesar? It was a tough choice for Christians. Nowhere else in Asia was this choice so painful, so costly, as in Pergamum. For this reason, Satan was probably on his throne at the temples of the emperors where this choice had to be made.

We know that Christians died for their faith here. In the letter to the church we read about Antipas, the faithful witness, who had been killed where Satan dwells.

But in spite of persecution, the Christians stood firm in their faith and the church grew, as this building shows. The Red Basilica is the largest ancient structure still standing in Pergamum. It's an immense building — the temple and courtyard nearly 700 feet long. It's made of brick, rather than stone, and was built in the second century as a temple to the Egyptian gods Isis and Serapis. But when persecution ended and the once-despised faith became popular, the Christians took over this temple about A.D. 400 and turned it into a church. And they named it in honor of John.

Now, let's go back to the acropolis and back to Revelation. Ian, tell us about the letter to the church here.

Ian Fair:

In His letter to Pergamum, Jesus commended the church for remaining true to Him even though Antipas was martyred where Satan's throne is [located].

In spite of the faithfulness of some in Pergamum, there were others who compromised their faith following the example of Balaam and Balak in the Old Testament. Like Israel, the compromise on Pergamum seemingly was in the practice of idolatry.

Christians of all ages will be tempted to compromise their faith, especially by trying to live in Christ and the world at the same time. The sharp warning to Pergamum was, "Repent then. If not, I will come to you soon and war against them with the sword of my mouth."

The reward of the faithful saints who conquered by dying without compromising their faith in Jesus was "hidden manna" or spiritual food that would sustain them forever.

Bill Humble:

This letter has some obvious warnings for our churches today. First, we are warned that a little compromise may open the floodgates of immorality. The Nicolaitans in the church probably began by arguing that they had to make a few concessions to Caesar. A pinch of incense at the altar, a few meaningless words — this was not too bad. But soon the Nicolaitans were into the worst immorality. Clement of Alexandria said that they abandoned themselves to pleasure like goats.

Another warning is that even when we confess our faith in words, we can deny it in how we live.

We don't choose between Christ and Caesar today. Our choices are more subtle. We have to choose between Christ and a culture that is saturated with sex and self-indulgence. Today, Satan's throne is everywhere — in the mass media, in our music and movies, even in the living room. Like the Christians at Pergamum, we do have to make a choice. And that choice is whether or not to follow Jesus as Lord in the way we live.

9

The Letter to Pergamum

Jesus' introduction of Himself as the one "who has the sharp two-edged sword" most likely draws on the fact that Pergamum was the seat of Roman senatorial government for the province of Asia. The symbol of the sword is a reminder of imperial authority. Jesus wants the church in Pergamum to remember that it is He who is Lord of lords — who holds ultimate authority and the power over life and death.

Pergamum was one of the leading cities of Asia. From here, the Roman proconsul presided over the province. In 29 B.C., the first temple of the imperial cult was built in Pergamum in honor of Rome and Emperor Augustus. The second largest temple and center for healing built in honor of Asklepios, the serpent god of healing, was located here. The impressive altar to the god Zeus was also in Pergamum. Situated on the summit of the mountain overlooking the city of Pergamum, the walled citadel posed an impressive sight — offering a magnificent view over the valleys and plains surrounding Pergamum. The power of Rome exuded from every nook and cranny of the city. Nevertheless, the Christians in Pergamum are reminded that this magnificent city is nothing more than the place of "Satan's throne."

Several possibilities in regard to the phrase "Satan's throne" have been suggested. One is that this is a reference to the altar to Zeus. Others believe that it is a reference to the temple to Asklepios. The third, and most likely explanation, is that it is a reference to the temple in honor of Rome and Augustus and the seat of Roman senatorial power. This is a reminder that the emperor, is not divine but human and demonic. Repeatedly in Revelation, this message will be made in a variety of symbols. One symbol is the reference to the Roman civil and imperial cult power as two beasts (Revelation 13). Another symbol is the number 666. Although this number has historically presented interpreters some difficulty, it is not that obscure. John tells us that this is a human number (Revelation 13:18). Therefore, it represents a human power, not a divine being. Christians should not worship the emperor under any conditions because he is a human being operating under a demonic or Satanic power, not a divine power. Jesus is Lord, not Caesar!

The impending persecution referred to by John in Revelation (1:1-3; 22:6,10) was already beginning. The Greek expression "at hand" or "is near" implies this urgency. At least one Christian in Pergamum, Antipas, had already given his life rather than compromise his faith.

Jesus acknowledges that the church in Pergamum is faithful, but follows this immediately with a reference to Balaam and Balak (Numbers 24:10ff; 31:15ff.) The "teaching of Balaam" is an allusion to Balaam's mercenary tendency to compromise. Jesus connects this immediately to "eating food sacrificed to idols" and the "practice of idolatry," followed by another reference to the immoral Nicolaitans.

Apparently, in contrast to the faithfulness of most in the church at Pergamum, there were some who were prone to compromise. They tempted others to follow suit, arguing that Christians are under grace and therefore free from all religious laws. It follows that although this compromise was in regard to foods, idolatry and immorality, this admonition should still be seen in the context of emperor worship at the imperial cult temples. Here one would also find immorality and food offered to idols associated with worshiping the emperor. Whatever the case, Balaam would be seen as a tendency to compromise one's faith in a pagan religious syncretism.

Temple of Trajan on the acropolis at Pergamum.

We know from the literature of the period that many Romans understood the emperor was merely human and not divine. Propriety, however, determined that it was easiest to fall in line with the culture and pay homage to the emperor as God. Unfortunately, some Christians followed suit, believing that to worship the emperor was merely a convention. Christians must always ensure that following convention does not lead them into a situation where they compromise their faith in Jesus.

Jesus' warning, "I will come to you soon," in the context of Revelation cannot be seen as a reference to His final, end of the world coming to judge the world in righteousness. Jesus, the one who is constantly walking around in the midst of His church (Revelation 2:1), comes constantly not only to encourage and strengthen His people, but also to judge them for an unrepentant heart. The language of Revelation is unique in its relating present reward and judgment to the final eschatologic judgment and reward. The intention of the eschatological language is to emphasize that Jesus' judgment on worldly Christians in Revelation comes with the full significance and weight of the final judgment.

In the letter to Pergamum, Jesus will "war against them" (judge them) with the "sword of His mouth." This is a typical Johannine expression stressing that Jesus' Word will judge us in the last day (John 12:44-50). To the martyrs Jesus will provide spiritual food in the form of "hidden manna". Rabbinic tradition held that the Messiah would provide his people with spiritual food as God through Moses had done during the Exodus (Exodus 16). In Revelation 2:7 the reward was "to eat of the tree of life." Jesus would ensure that those who died for Him would be sustained into eternal life.

The juxtapositioning of "hidden manna" and a "white stone" is fascinating. White stones would be given in a number of situations, common among them would be as an invitation to a banquet or wedding feast. On this stone would be written a new name which no one knows except him who receives it. Only the martyr would know the mystery or significance of this name. This name apparently signified a new character for the martyr; one that only the martyr and Jesus would know or understand. The reference seems to be that by dying with Jesus as a martyr — as Jesus had died for His faith — the martyr would share in the character of Jesus.

The reward promised the conqueror was one of sharing at the banquet of Jesus at the end of the world. This theme is repeated as the martyr's reward throughout the book of Revelation.

The message to Pergamum was to be careful — do not compromise your faith in any way with the pagan cults. The church could be characterized, therefore, as faithful yet with the tendency to compromise.

Christians today must be careful not to fall into the trap of believing that since grace abounds in Christ, one can compromise with the cultural niceties or conventions of society and still remain faithful to Jesus. Christianity is, in the words of John R.W. Stott — and in keeping with the Sermon on the Mount, a counter cultural way of life. Compromise steals up on one in a variety of forms and fashions. Christians must be alert to this. **IF**

Questions for Class Discussion

1. In what manner was the church in Pergamum impacted by its political, religious and secular environment?
2. In what environments might you find "Satan's throne" today?
3. What parallels can you identify between the church and Pergamum and being a Christian in the closing years of the 20th century?
4. How could people today be accused of holding to the "teaching of Balaam"?
5. Define antinomian. Discuss how we might be tempted to use grace as an excuse to do what we please rather than what pleases God.
6. How can we avoid the temptation to compromise? List some practical, real-life helps.
7. Discuss the meaning of the phrase, "Christianity is a counter cultural way of life."

10

SARDIS AND LAODICEA

Bill Humble:

Ian Fair and I have been taking you for a visit to the seven churches of Asia, and we've come now to Sardis.

Most of the buildings that were here in New Testament times have not yet been excavated, but there is one exception. In 1962 archaeologists uncovered this large Roman civic center with a gymnasium and baths. It's called the Marble Hall.

Sardis was an inland city, fifty miles east of Smyrna. Long before the gospel came to Sardis, it was the most important city in Asia and ruled over the kingdom of Lydia — that included all the land from Ephesus to Pergamum. The Pactolus River ran through Sardis. When gold was discovered in the Pactolus, Sardis became the richest city in the world.

Its most famous king was Croesus, who reigned about 550 B.C., and we still remember his wealth in gold. We still say, "As rich as Croesus." But there's another story about Croesus that you might remember. He was wanting to make war against the Persians, so he went to the oracle at Didyma — where we were — and asked the oracle if he should make war. The oracle said, "If you do, you will destroy a kingdom." He assumed that he would destroy the Persians, but instead it was his kingdom that he destroyed.

The Persians, under King Cyrus, laid siege to Sardis. But the city's acropolis was on a jagged peak — 1,500 feet high — and Croesus felt secure inside the walls. Then one day, as a Persian soldier watched, a Sardian soldier accidentally dropped his helmet off the wall and then climbed down through a narrow crevice to retrieve it. That crevice doomed Sardis. That night, with no sentries on watch, Persian soldiers slipped through the crevice and the city fell.

In the Lord's letter to Sardis, He warned the church twice to wake up or He would come like a thief — this may be an allusion to the time when the city was not watchful and Cyrus destroyed it.

Sardis would never again be as strong or wealthy, but it was still an important city in New Testament times — with a population of 100,000 and many beautiful buildings, including the Marble Hall.

Over the last thirty years, a great deal of archaeological work and restoration work has been done here. Look, for example, at this magnificent column with the spiral fluting going around it. This column is at least forty or fifty feet high, one solid piece of marble, magnificent work.

Husnu, what was the purpose of this Marble Hall?

Husnu Ovacik:
. This is a gymnasium — a third century one — and we have the *palestra* in front of this gymnasium, a large square [where] all kinds of sporting events took place. This Marble Hall was made for the emperor or the royal family to watch the events there. Also, they had this large swimming pool behind the Marble Hall.

Bill Humble:
This was built after an earthquake hit Asia in A.D. 17. Twelve cities were devastated, but Sardis suffered the worst damage. The destruction was so bad the Emperor Tiberius gave them generous help and remitted all taxes for five years. The Marble Hall was erected during this rebuilding after the earthquake, and it was enlarged in the third century.

The *palestra* is the large open area, surrounded by columns, where the athletic games were played. The Marble Hall has some of the most beautiful marble decorations that we have seen anywhere in Asia. Look at

Sites at Sardis

Top: Marble Hall, excavated and restored in the 1960's.

Center: Athletic Field. Acropolis of the city seen in background.

Bottom: Largest ancient Jewish synagogue ever discovered.

this spiral fluting — so perfect as it curves around the column, and the intricate designs on the architrave and the columns.

The Marble Hall also had training rooms and baths for the athletes who trained and played games in the *palestra*. In 1963 archaeologists uncovered a large room next to the Marble Hall. They discovered that it was a Jewish synagogue, the largest ancient synagogue ever found. The building had originally been a part of the Marble Hall, but sometime around A.D. 200 it began to be used as a synagogue. About a century later it was enlarged and a colonnaded courtyard was added on the east. The synagogue and courtyard together are more than 300 feet long.

The synagogue was richly decorated. The walls were covered with multi-colored marble. The floors, even in the courtyard, were made of mosaics. Many of these are still in place. Over eighty Jewish inscriptions were found, some of these in the mosaic floor. One inscription has the Hebrew word *shalom*. A marble table, perhaps a reading desk, is decorated with eagles, and lions stands nearby. A synagogue of this size and beauty means that thousands of Jews lived in Sardis.

Ian, that raises a question. Two of the seven letters, Smyrna and Philadelphia, reflect bitter hostility between the Jews and Christians. But there's none of that in the letter to Sardis. With so many Jews here, why not?

Ian Fair:

It's probably because the church here was not as faithful as the other two. The Lord told the church in Sardis that they were dead, and that's strong language. They had probably lost their evangelistic fervor and had quit trying to convince the Jews that Jesus was the Messiah. Under those circumstances, the Jews had little reason to be hostile to the Christians.

Bill Humble:

Sardis has one very impressive monument from pre-Christian times, the Temple of Artemis. This temple was built on the same grand scale as the one at Ephesus. It was begun in the third century B.C. and was the fourth largest building in the Hellenistic world — over 300 feet long.

The temple had 78 columns. Look at the size of this drum from one of the columns that has fallen. The drum is about seven feet in diameter. The square hole in the middle was for an iron peg that held the drums in place on top of one another. And look at how perfect the fluting is.

When Sardis had the great earthquake in A.D. 17, the temple was buried under a landslide. Later, it was uncovered and they continued to work on it for another hundred years. But it was never finished, as you can see form these columns that have no fluting. Remember that the stone masons carved the fluting on columns after they were standing. So these two columns, 58 feet tall, were put up, but the masons were never able to add the fluting. Other columns do have the fluting and beautiful decorations around the base, much like the Temple of Apollo at Didyma.

We don't know whether the preaching of the gospel threatened the cult of Artemis here at Sardis like it did at Ephesus. Perhaps not, because the church was a little like the city of Croesus. It was to comfortable and secure and it needed to wake up.

Ian, tell us about the letter.

Ian Fair:
The Lord's letter to the church at Sardis indicates that the church was very much like the city and with unfortunate circumstances. They had enormous unfulfilled potential, but were spiritually lethargic and asleep.

The church had a name for being alive, but Jesus said it was dead. Spiritually, it was such a model of inoffensive Christianity that it was impossible to distinguish it from its worldly pagan neighbors. Jesus warned the church that unless it awoke from its spiritual lethargy, He would come upon it like a thief in the night.

But in spite of the general lethargy in the church, there were some who had not compromised their faith. Jesus says "they are worthy." Worthiness, in the context of Revelation, is a steadfast refusal to compromise one's faith with the world. In almost every church, no matter how far removed it is from the ideal, there are those who remain true to their king and are, therefore, worthy of Jesus.

This must be our goal — to refuse to compromise with a secular world so that we can be "worthy of Jesus."

Bill Humble:
Ian, we've come now to Laodicea, the seventh and last of the seven churches. What kind of a city was Laodicea?

Ian Fair:
This was a very wealthy, a very self-independent city. Unfortunately, the church and the members of the church took on the character of the city. This was a church that depended on its own wealth — a very self-reliant church — and because of that had some serious problems that it had to face.

Bill Humble:
Yes, Laodicea was a rich city. It was [located] in the Lycus River valley, 100 miles directly east of Ephesus. It lay on the main Roman road from Ephesus to Syria and the East. This allowed Laodicea to levy taxes on all the trade that moved across Asia. The region was also famous for its sheep and black wool clothing. So with taxes on trade and sheep, Laodicea became wealthy.

Very little archaeological work has been done at Laodicea. But even without excavations, many ruins can be identified.

The city had a stadium, a thousand feet long, that was built during the Roman period. It is easy to identify this stadium by its oval shape, even though the tiers of seats are still buried. We know from an inscription that this stadium was dedicated to the Emperor Vespasian in A.D. 79. This is the same Vespasian who began the siege of Jerusalem when the temple was destroyed in A.D. 70. We also know from a letter of Cicero that gladiatorial contests were held here in Laodicea as early as 50 B.C.

Laodicea also had a theater, actually two theaters. This is the larger one, and even though it has not been excavated, it is obvious that it is a theater. Many of the upper rows of seats are still in place. A monument stone, dedicated to the Emperor Hadrian and dated A.D. 136, was found here in the theater.

Husnu Ovacik:
We have two theaters which an still be seen. One is bigger than the other. They are all from the Roman period. From the way the *cavea* looked, we can understand that they were used for gladiator fights and other wild beast shows, as well as the plays.

Bill Humble:
Archaeologically, Laodicea is different from all the other six cities of Asia. The tell is barren, not buried under a modern city like Smyrna or Philadelphia. But it has not been excavated like Ephesus or Pergamum.

Husnu, we've seen the ruins of the stadium and theater, but they have not been excavated. I wonder why not.

Husnu Ovacik:
The city was constructed over and over again — in the Hellenistic period, in the Roman period, in the Byzantine period and in the Ottoman period. So the material here was used and reused again, leaving almost nothing important for the archaeologists. This is probably why it has not been excavated.

Bill Humble:
There's something else. When the people of Laodicea finally left this hill, about a hundred years ago, and built a new town at Denizli, they carried away most of the cut stone and used it in their new town.

Here, at the south end of the stadium, we have the base of Laodicea's water tower. This may be the most interesting building here. This is because of Jesus' warning to the church, "Because you are lukewarm, and neither hot nor cold, I will spew you out of my mouth." This tower may help us understand this warning. But before we examine the tower, let's leave Laodicea and go to the city of Hierapolis, six miles to the north.

There was a church here, and unlike Laodicea, the archaeologists have been busy here. They have found a large cemetery with 1,200 graves from Roman times. Many of them have inscriptions, so we know that some of these graves were of Christians.

Here's an interesting Christian site, the Martyrium of Philip. It was built in the fifty century to honor the death of Philip. But we're not sure which Philip died here, whether it was the apostle or the evangelist.

Hierapolis was most famous for the white mineral terraces near the city. Today, the Turkish name is Pamukkale, and this means "cotton castle." These snow-white terraces are far larger than the ones in Yellowstone National Park. It's now a popular resort, and people bathe in little pools on the terraces. The warm mineral water may be good for bathing, but it has a foul sickening taste. So when the Lord told Laodicea, "I will spew you out of my mouth," they probably thought instantly of the "cotton castle" which they would see in the distance.

Now, let's go back to the water tower at Laodicea. Laodicea did not have springs near the city, so they had to build an aqueduct to bring water from several miles away. Sections of the aqueduct are still standing, where it crossed the valley and connected with the tower. The water did not come from the terraces at Hierapolis — but there is evidence that the water had a high mineral content, just like the water at the terraces.

This small section of the water tower that is still standing is honeycombed with pipes, and they are all clogged with mineral deposits inside the pipes. Even the large aqueduct got clogged, and it had to have openings where it could be cleaned out.

Since Laodicea has not been excavated, there are interesting artifacts lying around on the ground. Ian, what is that you picked up?

Ian Fair:
As I was walking by the aqueduct that carries the water into the city from the hills in the background, I picked up this piece of clay pipe — what is interesting to

notice here is the mineral deposit on the inside of the clay pipe, indicating that the water that came into this community was full of mineral deposits and very distasteful.

Bill Humble:
Husnu, what are these minerals?

Husnu Ovacik:
This is obviously a brick piping, but the inside is almost plugged with the calcium carbonate deposits. In fact it's the same thing you have in your teapots.

Bill Humble:
So the people of Laodicea knew something about foul-tasting mineral water. When the Lord said, "I will spew you out of my mouth," they would have known exactly what He meant.

We have now come to a large gymnasium and bath complex next to the stadium and water tower. Several of the archways are still intact. An inscription has been found telling how this building was dedicated to the Emperor Hadrian when he visited here in A.D. 129 — only thirty or forty years after John wrote Revelation. So it's a good place for us to talk about the Lord's letter to the church here.

Ian Fair:
The letter to Laodicea was the last of the seven letters Jesus addressed to the church in Asia, and it is the one that has the most severe condemnation.

Perhaps no church of antiquity speaks more clearly to Christians in this century of affluent societies than does Laodicea. Laodicea was comfortable and secure in its wealth. Too often Christians today tend to measure greatness in terms of wealth, power and education. The real danger in which the Laodicean church found itself was that being lukewarm it did not know that it was neither hot nor cold. Christians who are cold know their spiritual condition. Being lukewarm is dangerous in that Christians do not know the seriousness of their condition. In the strongest terms, Jesus warns the Laodiceans to realize their real spiritual poverty and to do something to rectify this before He personally has to take drastic steps.

The greatest lesson we can learn from Laodicea is that without the richness of a deep spiritual relationship with God through Jesus, we are in abject poverty.

Bill Humble:
The Lord's letter to the church here in Laodicea is the only one that has only rebuke — no words of praise.

They said, "We are rich and need nothing," but the Lord said they were "wretched, pitiable, poor, blind and naked." They needed Him, and they didn't know it.

But with all its problems, the church did not die. Here is the evidence — an ancient church with some of the arches still sticking up out of the ground. We don't know when this church was built. But the history of the church in Laodicea seems to parallel the other churches of Asia. When Christianity became the state religion of the Roman empire, it grew rapidly and great churches were built. But the outward strength hid its inner weakness. When the Muslims conquered Asia in the seventh century, the churches withered and disappeared.

Today, two great buildings in Istanbul symbolize what happened to the church. The first is Hagia Sophia, an immense church built by Justinian in the sixth century. It is amazing that a building so large could have been built 1,400 years ago. Istanbul, or Constantinople, remained a Christian city for 800 years after Asia had fallen to the Muslims. But in 1453, Istanbul was conquered and Hagia Sophia became a mosque, with minarets added to the great church. But everyone knew that Christians had built Hagia Sophia, and the Muslims wanted to show that they could build its equal, so the Blue Mosque was constructed.

Today, these two buildings face one another. Hagia Sophia is a museum and the Christian faith is a relic of the past in Turkey — pushed aside by Islam and the mosque.

There is a lesson here. If our churches are to endure we must go back to the Word, heed the Lord's warnings to the seven churches, and proclaim by the way we live that "Jesus is Lord."

11

The Letter to Sardis

The Lord's message to the church in Sardis was harsh, "I know your works; you have the name of being alive, and you are dead" (Revelation 3:1). Sir William Ramsey observed that in the history of Sardis there was a "melancholy contrast" between its earlier greatness and its decay and degeneration by the first century. He saw the decay of the once great city reflected in the condition of the church (William Barclay, *The Revelation of John*, Philadelphia, Westminster Press, Vol. I, p. 113). Six centuries earlier Sardis had been the wealthiest and strongest city in Asia Minor, but by New Testament times its past glory was a distant memory — though some of the old wealth was still there. Similarly, the earlier spiritual vitality of the church had waned. Now, they had a reputation for being an active church, but in Jesus' eyes they were dead.

What had brought the church to this sad state? The problems that were so serious among the other churches are missing in this letter. This letter says nothing about the temptation to go along with pagan sacrifices and immorality, unless the reference to the few who had not soiled their garments implies that most disciples at Sardis were stained with immorality. There is no warning about the Nicolaitans, whose teachings plagued Ephesus and Pergamum. Sardis had no Jezebel calling for compromise with immoral pagan rituals.

Emperor worship doesn't seem to be a problem to the disciples in Sardis either. No brother or sister had become a faithful martyr at Satan's throne. There isn't any evidence of Jewish hostility like that their fellow Christians at Smyrna and Philadelphia faced. Yet we know that Sardis had a large and wealthy Jewish community, for archaeologists have uncovered and restored the largest ancient synagogue ever found.

So without Nicolaitans, a Jezebel, Jewish threats or persecution because of emperor worship, the church in Sardis was drifting along with a reputation for being alive. In reality it was dead. The church was meeting on the Lord's day and going through the motions of being a church, but genuine spirituality and commitment had long since waned. Maintaining an outward reputation for piety and faithfulness, the church had sunk into spiritual apathy. Jesus declared, "I have not found your works perfect in the sight of my God."

And yet, there were rays of hope for this dead church. The Lord told them, in four commands, how they could be transformed into the kind of church they were reputed to be. The Lord told them first to "awake" or "be watchful." This call to watchfulness should have reminded the Sardians of the two dark hours in their city's past when it had fallen because its army was not vigilant. The Persians had besieged their city, about 55 B.C., when Croesus was king. Because Sardis stood atop an acropolis 1,500 feet high it seemed impregnable and sentries seemed unnecessary. King Cyrus of Persia offered a large reward to anyone who could find a breach in the defenses. A Persian soldier saw a Sardian defender accidentally drop his helmet off the battlement, then slip down through a crevice to retrieve it. That night, with no Sardians on guard, the Persian led an assault through the narrow crevice and earned Cyrus' reward. Three centuries later in 218 B.C., Sardis fell again, this time to Antiochus, because no sentries were watching.

Jesus' second command was to "strengthen what remains and is on the point of death." All was not yet lost, even though the church was in critical condition. There was still a flicker of life, but the church had to act quickly to rekindle the flame.

The third command was to "remember then what you received and heard" and keep it. We know nothing about how the church began in Sardis, but because Jesus wanted them to remember what they had heard there must have been something special about the first proclamation of the Good News in Sardis. If they would now keep that message, they would be on the way back to life.

"Repent," the fourth command, summarized it all. When a church is dying, its only hope is an about-face in its attitude toward the Lord and in its commitment to His way of life. If the church does not repent, then Jesus will come "like a thief." This analogy between the thief and the unexpectedness of judgment is found many times in the New Testament (Matthew 24:42-44; 2 Peter 3:10).

Despite the melancholy state of the Sardis church as a whole, Jesus knew there were "a few names in Sardis, people who have not soiled their garments, and they shall walk with me in white, for they are worthy" (Revelation 3:4). The faithful remnant in a dead church like Sardis should be an encouragement to any Christian today who finds himself in a similar situation. It is easy to become discouraged when one's congregation is apathetic, without real zeal for serving or evangelizing. Or perhaps the church is so plagued by squabbling brethren that one can feel the tension when he should be worshiping the Father in joyous love. It is always tempting, given such circumstances, to slip quietly away to another congregation. Sometimes this may be the best course to follow. But it is comforting to know that when people remain faithful to Jesus in a dying or divided church, Jesus knows who they are and promises that they will walk in fellowship with Him.

The letter ends with three promises to the one who "conquers" — the familiar word found at the end of all seven letters. First, he will be clothed in white garments. This is in stark contrast with the soiled garments worn by most Sardian Christians. White has always been a symbol of purity, but in the ancient world it was also the color of victory. When Rome celebrated a successful campaign, its citizens appeared at the parade in white and Rome was "the city of white." Second, his name will not be blotted out of the book of life. As Greco-Roman cities kept registers of citizens, so God has a book of life recording the names of those who belong to Him. Third, Jesus will confess his name before the Father, a promise identical to one Jesus had made during His earthly ministry (Matthew 10:32-33).

No other church among the seven, except Laodicea, had declined as low as Sardis in its spiritual life. But there was hope that the faithful remnant might lead the congregation in spiritual renewal. The road to renewal would be hard — demanding repentance, watchfulness, and keeping the message they had received — but those who followed this road would conquer.   **BH**

Questions for Class Discussion

1. How did the church in Sardis reflect the city?

2. What forces tempt us to be complacent today?

3. What were the signs of spiritual decline in Sardis?

4. Do you know of churches or people today that have a reputation for being spiritually alive but are really dead? What are some of the tell-tale signs of such decline?

5. What were the Lord's commands for bringing Sardis back to life? How does each apply today?

6. If you were one of the faithful few in a church like Sardis, what would you do about it?

7. What practical lessons can we learn from the letter to Sardis?

12

The Letter to Laodicea

The church in Laodicea had the dismal distinction of receiving Jesus' only letter that had nothing but rebuke and warning — not a single word of commendation or praise. Even dead Sardis had a faithful remnant who would walk in fellowship with Jesus — but not Laodicea.

The "faithful and true" Jesus came straight to the heart of Laodicea's moral problem in the oft-quoted rebuke, "I know your works: you are neither cold nor hot. Would that you were cold or hot! So, because you are lukewarm, and neither cold nor hot, I will spew you out of my mouth" (Revelation 3:15-16). The lukewarm disciple is in a precarious spiritual condition because he is oblivious to his plight. The Christian who has become "cold" knows where he is. Although he is unwilling to repent and return to the Lord, he knows exactly where he is and what he needs to do. The lukewarm Laodiceans did not know where they were. Laodicea was a wealthy city, and the Christians shared the prosperity. The church said smugly, "I am rich, I have prospered, and I need nothing." But in Jesus' eyes they were "wretched, pitiable, poor, blind, and naked." Tragically they did not know it.

The first beatitude says, "Blessed are the poor in spirit, for theirs is the kingdom of heaven" (Matthew 5:3). The poor in spirit are those who are acutely aware of their spiritual poverty and their total dependence on God. There was none of this among the Laodiceans. Their affluence in material things blinded them to the poverty of their spirits. Like the rich fool, they had it made financially, but they were not rich toward God. Wealth often works this way. The New Testament warns that wealth is frequently a threat to discipleship. "It is easier for a camel to go through the eye of a needle than for a rich man to enter the kingdom of God" (Luke 18:25). Our churches today need to hear this warning. We too are rich — far richer than we realize — and this is when we become susceptible to lukewarmness.

Smyrna and Laodicea present a striking contrast. The Christians in Smyrna were in poverty, but because they knew their need for the Lord they were rich. The Laodiceans lived in wealth, but because they trusted in that wealth they were in spiritual poverty.

The lukewarm Laodiceans made Jesus so sick that He threatened, "I will spew [vomit] you out of my mouth." Strong, arresting language — bringing vivid images to the Laodiceans. They knew about the great white mineral terraces at Hierapolis, a New Testament city a few miles to the north. Today an important Turkish resort, Pamukkale, has grown up around the terraces. Pamukkale means "cotton castle," and that's what the white terraces looked like from Laodicea. They knew that the warm mineral water was great for healing baths, but nauseating to drink. They also knew that their own city water supply, brought from the south by aqueduct, was from warm springs with high mineral content. Part of the city water tower is still standing with the pipes that carried water through the city, and many of those pipes are badly clogged with minerals. Lukewarm mineral water that makes one sick enough to vomit — the Laodiceans knew what this meant, and Jesus said that's what they were.

Jesus called on the Laodiceans to realize their need for Him, and His three calls focused on areas of life where they were most self-assured and self-satisfied. First, He counseled them to buy gold from Him. As noted earlier, Laodicea was a wealthy city. It was in a rich agricultural area, and Laodicea commanded the trade routes across Asia. When 12 Asian cities were destroyed by an earthquake in 17 B.C., Laodicea accepted help from Emperor Tiberius to rebuild. But when it was destroyed again in A.D. 61, the city was wealthy enough to rebuild without Roman aid. They had the gold that came from mining and trade, but Jesus said they needed the riches that only He could bring.

Jesus' second call to Laodicea was to buy white garments from Him to cover their nakedness. They had the finest clothing anywhere, and everyone knew it. The Lycus River valley was famous for its sheep with glossy-black wool. Clothing made from this wool was expensive and highly prized. But these well-clad Laodiceans stood before their Lord spiritually naked.

"The shame of your nakedness" would have meant more to ancient people than it does today. To be stripped naked was the ultimate humiliation. The British Museum has many Assyrian sculptures showing enemy soldiers, whom had been captured in battle, being paraded naked before their captors. The Old Testament prophets often threatened God's disobedient people with nakedness, as in Nahum 3:5, "I will let the nations look on your nakedness." Jesus could see the Laodiceans' nakedness of heart, even if they couldn't.

Jesus' third call was for them to buy salve to anoint their eyes so that they could see. Just west of Laodicea, there was a temple to the god Men which had a medical school noted for using collyrium in treating eye diseases. We have writings of Galen, the famous physician who took his training at the Aesclepion in Pergamum, describing the use of this medicine. The Laodiceans thought they were curing the blindness of others, but they were blind to their own blindness.

Arches of ancient church at Laodicea.

Why did Jesus use such strong language in addressing these poor, naked, blind, lukewarm disciples? He answers, "Those whom I love, I reprove and chasten."

The letter ends with one of the most appealing pictures of Jesus found anywhere in Scripture. "Behold, I stand at the door and knock; if any one hears my voice and opens the door, I will come in to him and eat with him; and he with me." The imagery may be taken from the Song of Solomon 5:2-6, where the lover pleads with his beloved to open the door.

What is unique in this picture of Jesus is that God is seeking man. William Barclay has noted that no other religion has this vision of a seeking God. Barclay tells about a National Christian Council which met in Japan to ask what made Christianity different from all other religions. The Council found Christianity's uniqueness in "man not seeking God, but God taking the initiative in seeking man" (William Barclay, *The Revelation of John*, Philadelphia, Westminster Press, Vol. I, p. 147).

The seeking Lord inspired artist Holman Hunt to paint his famous picture, "The Light of the World." The night is dark and there is blackness everywhere. The lonely traveler, carrying a small lantern whose light barely penetrates the gloom, comes to a small cabin. He stands knocking patiently at the door. As viewers study the picture, they suddenly realize that the door has no latch on the outside. It can only be opened from the inside.

The more affluent people become the more they need to listen to Jesus' beatitude, "Blessed are the poor in spirit." We, like the Laodiceans, have been blessed with far more than our share of the good things of life. The danger is that this will blind us to our need for God, and we will become as spiritually poverty-stricken as the Laodiceans. Jesus is the Good Shepherd who seeks us. He wants us to be His disciples. He stands at the door knocking, but He will never force His way into our hearts. We have to open that door. **BH**

Questions for Class Discussion

1. Why is spiritual lukewarmness so dangerous?
2. Do you think that our affluence is a threat to our spirituality? If so, what can we do about it?
3. If you were trying to decide whether a congregation was drifting into spiritual lukewarmness, what symptoms would you look for?
4. How does the American ideal of self-sufficiency compare with Jesus' call for dependence on Him?
5. How did Jesus' three calls challenge the Laodiceans sense of self-sufficiency? How would Jesus call us in a similar way?

6. How has God taken the initiative in seeking you out?
7. What practical lessons for churches today can you find in this letter?

Epilogue

Ephesus was steadfast, but lacked love. Smyrna was persecuted. Pergamum was willing to compromise their faith. Thyatira was willing to tolerate immorality. Sardis had become apathetic. Philadelphia was patiently serving God. Laodicea was self-sufficient and forgot its need for God.

These are the very same conditions that the church can find itself in today. While we are not faced with emperor worship, we are pressured daily to focus our attention on idols rather than God. The warnings given to those who are materially rich speak especially loudly to us today. We are reminded that we have no hope apart from God's grace. Yet grace does not give us a right to do as we please. God demands moral and doctrinal purity. He also demands that all things be done out of love for Him and with love towards our fellow man.

The messages of Revelation 2-3 needed to be heard by the early church. They need to be heard by the church today. They will be needed by the church tomorrow. Why? Because there is a battle going on between God and Satan. God wants all people to be with Him in heaven, but Satan is determined to lead man away from God. God has left the choice of whom to serve up to each one of us.

The book of Revelation reminds us, as it reminded early Christians, that the final outcome of this struggle has already been determined. That outcome, and the main message of Revelation, can be summed up in three statements:

> God is in control.
> Be faithful.
> His people will be victorious.